英検®合格
のための

要約問題
予想問題集

英検® **1級**/準**1級**/**2級** 対応

学研プライムゼミ特任講師
竹岡広信 著

Gakken

はじめに

検定試験の対策の意味とは

　昔、普段教えている高校1年生が、英検®（実用英語技能検定）2級の面接を受けるので、その訓練をして欲しいと相談に来たことがあります。私はその生徒に対して、「検定試験というものは、君の現在の英語力を測るためのものだ。確かに直前対策をすれば、合格する可能性が少しは高まるかもしれないが、そのようなことをして受かっても何の意味があるというのか？　何の対策もしないまま合格すれば、君がその基準に達していることになるし、もし落ちたならば、それから日々精進すればいいじゃないか」と言いました。その生徒はがっくり肩を落として「わかりました」と言って帰って行きました。客観的に見れば、私は「酷い教師」に映ったかもしれません。しかし、そのような安直な「対策」で受かってしまう試験に何の意味があるのでしょうか？

検定試験はゲームのようなもの！？

　そもそも、検定試験は、どんな形式の問題でもパターン化されてしまうことが多いものです。よっていかなる形式のものでも、「対策」がなされる傾向があります。書店の英語本コーナーに行ってみてください。「○×対策問題集」「10日間で完成○×問題集」などの本が所狭しと並べられています。まるでゲームの攻略本のような感じがしますね。TOEIC®などに熱狂している人がいるのもうなずけます。大学受験は、多くの人にとって1回や2回のチャンスしかありません。ところが検定試験は、年に何回も受験ができるだけでなく、何回受験してもよいわけです。極端に言えば、100回以上受験しても（大学受験なら100浪ということはあり得ませんが）誰にも文句は言われません。

英作文に要約を出すことの意義

　従来の英検®（実用英語技能検定）の英作文も、そのようなパターン化されたものの1つでした。英検®の英作文対策本は、出題される可能性がある英作文のトピックを取り上げ、その模範解答を示し、受験生はそれを忠実に暗記するというものでした。本番の試験で、お題を見た瞬間に、覚えてきた英語を記憶から引っ張り出し、一切考えることなく、それを答案用紙に記入する、という人が多かった気がします。2024年度からのリニューアルで「要約」が出題され、「パターン化」が難しくなり、本当の英語力を試す問題に近づきました。よって本書も、本当に英語の力をつけるための指南書を目指しました。皆さんは、本書を用いて、ただ黙々と要約に取り組み「本物の力」の向上のために努力してください。

竹 岡 広 信

もくじ

本 書 の 使 い 方

　本書は英検1級、準1級、2級に出題される「要約問題」対策の問題集です。2級レベル10問、準1級レベル10問、1級レベル5問、合計25問の予想問題トレーニングを通して、英検に合格するための「読解力」と「要約力」が養えます。ここでは本書の特長と使い方を紹介します。

問 題 編

　まずは別冊の要約問題にチャレンジしましょう。2級（10問）、準1級（10問）、1級（5問）とレベルごとにステップアップする形で問題を掲載しています。

❶問題　過去問を徹底分析し、長文のテーマを厳選し英文を作成。モニター検証、ネイティブチェックを経て練り上げたオリジナル問題を収録しています。

❷解答欄　日本英語検定協会が公表している解答用紙サンプルをもとに作った「解答欄」です。解答欄の枠内に解答を収めることが採点を受ける必要条件なので、本番のつもりで答案を書き込んでみましょう。

解答・解説

　別冊の問題を解き終わったら、本冊の「解答例と解説」に進み、ポイントを確認しましょう。答え合わせだけでなく、次のSTEPに従って解説を読み、英文の要点を正しくつかみ、うまく英語で要約できたかを確認しましょう。

STEP1　問題文の要点をつかむ

　問題英文を段落ごとに再掲し、日本語訳、語彙リストのあとに、英文の内容を吟味し、何を要約文に含めるべきかをくわしく解説しています。含めるべき内容を❶、❷などの番号で明示し、竹岡先生独自の採点基準を示しています。

STEP2　モニター答案でポイントをつかむ

　巻頭の本書オリジナルの採点基準に沿って、竹岡先生が実際に添削をしたモニター答案を掲載しています。1つの問題につき、2つの答案例があり、いずれも受験者のみなさんが陥りがちなミスを含むものです。添削と竹岡先生のコメントを読んで、ポイントをしっかりつかみましょう。

STEP3　ネイティブスピーカーの答案に学ぶ

　最後にStephen Richmond先生による「模範解答」を掲載しています。ネイティブスピーカーが英文をどう読み、どう要約したかの一例として参照してください。STEP 1やSTEP 2で示した内容を必ずしも満たしていないものもありますが、ネイティブスピーカーが要約する際に駆使している「言い換え」や構文のテクニックを学び、1ランク上の答案を目指しましょう。

本 書 で 使 用 し て い る 主 な 記 号

動＝動詞　名＝名詞　副＝副詞　形＝形容詞　接＝接続詞　前＝前置詞

熟＝熟語　S＝主語　V＝動詞　O＝目的語　C＝補語

英 文 要 約 の 心 得

1 . 課 題 と な る 英 文 を し っ か り 理 解 す る こ と !

　要約問題は「英文解釈能力」を問う問題でもあります。当然のことですが、課題となる英文の内容を理解していることが、要約する際の大前提です。課題文を「だいたいしか理解できていない」というレベルでは、要約などできるはずがありません。従来の英文解釈の問題と同様に、まず課題文をしっかり読み理解してください。もし可能なら、段落ごとに簡単なメモをして、頭の中を整理しながら英文を読み進めてください。

　「はやく要約しなければ」と焦るあまり、課題文である英文を適当に読んでしまっている人は意外と多いのです。

2 . 「 何 が 言 い た い 英 文 な の か 」 の 方 針 を 立 て る こ と !

　各段落の細かいポイントを云々する前に、英文全体を読んで「結局この英文は何が言いたいのか」を考えてください。その方向性を間違えると大幅に減点されるどころか、場合によっては0点になる可能性さえあります。「木を見て森を見ず」ではダメだということです。たとえば、「アジアゾウの絶滅危機の原因は、ゾウの居住地減少によって、ゾウが人間と接触したことだ」という主張の文があったとします。この要約を「アジアゾウを救わねばならない」という方向で書いた場合、相当な減点がなされます。とにかく課題文である英文を精読して、その英文の「一番言いたいこと」をしっかり考えてください。特に1級では、「全体を俯瞰する力」が求められていますから、とにかく英文の言いたいことに注意を注いでください。

3 . 各 段 落 で の ポ イ ン ト を 考 え る こ と !

　2でも述べた通り、「何が言いたい英文なのか」を理解することは極めて重要ですが、それだけでは十分ではありません。答案を採点していると、ざっと読んだあと、自分が覚えている印象だけを頼りに、何となく要約文を書いたものをよく見かけます。フィーリングだけで解答を書くというのは、本当にありがちなのですが、残念ながらそれでは高得点は望めません。各段落の1文1文を吟味して、それぞれの文のつながりを考え、書くべき内容を頭を振り絞って考えてください。たとえば次の文の言いたいことは何でしょうか。

Space exploration has long been a worldwide effort to explore the potential of the universe. When many people hear the term "space exploration," they think of rocket launches, space stations, and so on. However, what exactly is being done is probably not well known to most people.

「宇宙探査は昔から、宇宙の可能性を探る世界的な取り組みであった。『宇宙探査』という言葉を聞くと、ロケットの打ち上げや宇宙ステーションなどを思い浮かべる人が多いだろう。しかし、正確にどのようなことが行われているのかは、大半の人におそらくあまり知られていない」

この英文は「宇宙探査」に対する、一般的な人の認識が述べられています。筆者の主張はHowever 以降の、「ほとんどの人は、宇宙探査がどのようなものかを正確に知らない（Most people do not know exactly what space exploration involves.）」となります。

4．課題文の英文は極力借用しないこと！

「英文要約」の試験では、当然ですが、皆さんの「英作文力」も試されています。特に2級レベルの生徒の答案を採点していると、「英文要約」を「該当箇所を借用してそれを丸写しすること」と勘違いしているようなものに多数出合います。「言い換えた結果、間違った表現になった」というのも避けたいですが、自分が現在持っている自信のある英語表現を駆使してできるだけ言い換えてください。もっともシンプルなのはparticipate in ～「～に参加する」をtake part in ～に言い換えるといったものです。Tall buildings in big cities block the wind. を The wind is blocked by tall buildings.「風は高層ビルによって遮られている」のような、能動態から受動態への変換といった単純なものも時にはOKですが、英文の構造全体を変えてしまうような高レベルの言い換えが必要な時もあります。どのように言い換えるかに「一定のパターン」はないので、本書での演習を通じて徐々に身につけていただければ幸いです。

5．ミスのない英文を書くこと！

書き終えた後の「見直しルーティーン」を作っておくといいでしょう。動詞は、現在形の場合「三人称単数現在のs」は必要かどうか。名詞は、「単数形か複数形か、あるいは冠詞は必要かどうか」などのチェック項目を作っておくのです。料理の味付けの順番が、「さ（砂糖）」、「し（塩）」、「す（酢）」、「せ（醤油）」、「そ（味噌）」であるように、見直しの順を決めておくことが重要なのです。基本的なミスを「ケアレスミス」と言っているようでは、上級者の仲間入りをするのは困難です。「ミスは絶対にしてはいけない」という決意が必要です。

150語前後の英文を読み、その内容を45語から55語の英文で要約する問題です。

出題サンプルを分析すると、問題英文は3段落構成の論説文で、最初の段落で文章全体のテーマを提示し、続く第2・第3段落では第1段落であげたテーマのメリットとデメリットを述べるという構成です。2級全体の出題範囲を加味すると、要約問題の長文のトピックは学校生活や友人関係、日常的あるいは社会的な関心事など、比較的身近な内容のものが多くなると予想されます。

- 以下の英文を読んで、その内容を<u>英語で要約し</u>、解答欄に記入しなさい。
- 語数の目安は45語〜55語です。
- 解答欄の外に書かれたものは採点されません。
- 解答が英文の要約になっていないと判断された場合は、<u>0点と採点されることがあります</u>。英文をよく読んでから答えてください。

テーマの提示

　　Students used to use either paper or electronic dictionaries when they studied a foreign language, but nowadays many do not use either option. Instead, they use online dictionaries.

メリット

　　What are the reasons for this? Online dictionaries are most accessible because most students have a smartphone and they can easily access the Internet through it. Online dictionaries are much lighter and cheaper than the other two. Students can listen to the proper pronunciation of words, too.

デメリット

　　Needless to say, there are some disadvantages to online dictionaries as well. Depending on the Wi-Fi connection, the students may not be able to access them.　Most importantly, if the students often use online dictionaries, they will become dependent on them and no longer voluntarily learn new words. They may get distracted by phone calls, emails, videos, and entertainment apps. As a result, they may not be able to focus on studying.

要約のポイント

　ポイントは解答が英文の「要約」になっていること、つまり問題文から適当な英文をそのまま抜き出すのではなく、英文の要点をつかんだ上で、過不足なく簡潔な文章にまとめることです。具体例として挙げられている事柄を総称的・抽象的な言葉で言い換える力も必要になるでしょう。もちろん45語から55語という語数制限を厳守するのが大前提です。

　英検本番では「内容」「構成」「語彙」「文法」の4つの観点で採点されることが公表されていますが、本書では「内容（構成も含む）」と「文法（語彙も含む）」の解説に焦点をあてるため、「内容点」「文法点」の2つの観点から右のような本書独自の採点基準を設定しています。

本 書 で の 採 点 基 準 （2 級）

※この基準は本書独自のもので、公益財団法人 日本英語検定協会が公表しているものではありません。

1. 語 数 に つ い て

45 語未満の場合（不足1語につき）	1点減点
45 語〜55 語	減点なし
55 語を超える場合（過剰1語につき）	1点減点

2. 文 法 に つ い て

軽度の間違い	1点減点
重大な間違い	2〜3点減点

[軽度の間違いの例]

1）大文字・小文字の間違い　[例] Because..., × He [→he] is ....
2）句読点の間違い　[例] We were surprised at the news [→. のヌケ]
3）元の単語が推測できるレベルの綴りの間違い
　　[例] × grammer [→ grammar]
　　ただし、同じ単語の綴りのミスは、2回目は減点しないものとする。
4）名詞の単数・複数の間違い　[例] I like × a dog [→ dogs].
5）冠詞の間違い　[例] × a [→an] important role
6）三単現のsの脱落　[例] She × like [→likes] cats.

[重大な間違いの例]

7）不要なものを追加した間違い、必要なものが脱落する間違い
　　[例] discuss × about [→トル] it, the room I work [→ work in]
8）品詞の間違い　[例] × some of people [→some people]
9）語法、コロケーションの間違い　[例] the habit × to smoke [→of smoking]

3. 引 用 に つ い て

● 本文を10語以上連続してそのまま引用している場合、その文の内容点は与えないものとする。

4. 内 容 に つ い て

● 本書では満点を25点とする。問題文の趣旨を理解していないと思われるものは25点減点とする。
● 採点は減点法とする。具体的な得点は各問題の解説で明示する。
● ただし適切な接続詞が落ちている場合は2〜3点減点する。

200語前後の英文を読み、その内容を60語から70語の英文で要約する問題です。

出題サンプルを分析すると、問題英文は3段落構成の論説文で、最初の段落で文章全体のテーマを提示し、続く第2・第3段落では第1段落であげたテーマのメリットとデメリットを述べるという構成です。準1級全体の出題範囲を勘案すると、要約問題の長文のトピックは社会・環境・教育・化学・ビジネス・IT・メディアなど多岐に渡ると予想されます。

- Instructions: Read the article below and summarize it in your own words as far as possible in English.
- Suggested length: 60-70 words
- Write your summary in the space provided on your answer sheet. <u>Any writing outside the space will not be graded.</u>

テーマの提示

In 2013, public transportation became free in Tallinn, the capital of Estonia. Before that, free public transportation initiatives had been implemented only in relatively small municipalities and never in a capital city. Under the initiative, only registered residents can purchase a "green card" for two euros, and with that, all buses, streetcars, and trolleybuses in the city are free of charge.

メリット

These initiatives were expected to bring benefits, such as increased tax revenues due to a population increase for free rides, reduced equipment costs for railway companies, contributing to a better environment due to reduced number of cars, and improved mobility for low-income people.

デメリット

According to a 2014 survey, it is true that the number of times Tallinn residents walked on foot decreased by 40%. However, the number of times they traveled by car decreased by only 5%. Apparently, the effect on gas emissions was not as large as had been expected. And of course, this does not seem to be suitable for every city. For example, in Paris, France, there are many people who oppose the idea of free fares, believing that it would simply lead to a reduction in fare revenues, which would ultimately increase the burden on taxpayers.

要約のポイント

要約のポイントは問題冒頭のInstructionsにある通り、できるだけ「自分の言葉」で要約する、つまり問題文からそのまま抜き出すのではなくパラフレーズしてまとめることです。2級に比べて英文には具体的な数字や固有名詞が多く含まれているので、こうした要素のうち

何を要約に盛り込み、何を省くかの見極めが重要です。もちろん60語から70語という語数制限を厳守することが鉄則です。

　英検本番では「内容」「構成」「語彙」「文法」の4つの観点で採点されることが公表されていますが、本書では「内容（構成も含む）」と「文法（語彙も含む）」の解説に焦点をあてるため、「内容点」「文法点」の2つの観点から下記のような本書独自の採点基準を設定しています。

本書での採点基準（準1級）

※この基準は本書独自のもので、公益財団法人 日本英語検定協会が公表しているものではありません。

1. 語数について

60語未満の場合（不足1語につき）	1点減点
60語〜70語	減点なし
70語を超える場合（過剰1語につき）	1点減点

2. 文法について

軽度の間違い	大文字・小文字の間違い／句読点の間違い／元の単語が推測できるレベルの綴りの間違い*／冠詞のヌケ・間違い*／名詞の単数・複数の間違い／三単現のsの脱落など	1点減点
重大な間違い	to不定詞か動名詞か／自動詞か他動詞か／時制の不一致／接続詞や前置詞の誤用／不可算名詞、複数形名詞の所有格のような、文法・語法上の誤り／主語または目的語の欠落、あるいは重文・複文の接続詞の脱落のような、構文上の間違い	2〜3点減点

※roleをrollとするなど意味が変わってしまう綴りのミスは2点減点。※先行詞の前の冠詞のミスは2点減点。
※1文中で、ある誤りが2語以上に及ぶ場合でも、明らかにそれが1つの誤りに帰すると思われる場合には1回の減点にとどめるものとする。※someoneなどの不定代名詞を受ける代名詞に関しては、性差別を避ける観点から、he or sheまたはtheyとするのが一般的であるが、he / his / himを減点しないものとする。※同じ単語については重複して減点しない。

3. 引用について

- 本文の文を5語以上連続してそのまま引用している場合、その文の内容点は与えないものとする。
- ただし固有名詞あるいはそれに準ずる名詞においては減点しないものとする。

4. 内容について

- 本書では満点を25点とする。問題文の趣旨を理解していないと思われるものは25点減点とする。
- 採点は減点法とする。具体的な得点は各問題の解説で明示する。
- ただし論理的な整合性に欠ける文（[例]根拠・理由に結論との整合性がないもの、常識の範囲で理由とは認められないもの）は各2〜3点減点する。

1 級 の 要 約 問 題

300語程度の英文を読み、その内容を90語から110語の英文で要約する問題です。

出題サンプルを分析すると、問題英文は3段落構成の論説文で、第1段落でテーマが提示されたあと、テーマに関する事例や詳しい説明が第2段落と第3段落でなされています。2級や準1級のように「テーマ提示→メリット→デメリット」のような構成ではないため、段落ごとにしっかり要旨をとらえることが重要です。1級全体の出題範囲を加味すると、長文のトピックは社会・環境・教育・化学・ビジネス・IT・メディアなど多岐に渡ると予想されます。

- Instructions: Read the article below and summarize it in your own words as far as possible in English.
- Suggested length: 90-110 words
- Write your summary in the space provided on your answer sheet. Any writing outside the space will not be graded.

Sea reclamation projects in Bahrain, where the seabed is used to build new islands, have been carried out mainly along the coastline since the 1960s, expanding the country from 690 square km to over 780 square km by 2021—making Bahrain today slightly larger in area than Singapore. Neighboring Gulf states with even larger land areas have also been building large-scale artificial islands for decades. Some are especially striking, such as Palm Jumeirah in Dubai, which started being constructed in 1990. It is now a group of offshore islands that together resemble a palm tree and are home to luxury hotels.

Meanwhile, experts studying the history of artificial island construction are concerned about the impact of projects to reclaim the sea and build islands. This is because these artificial islands are often built on coral reefs that are home to hundreds of tropical species. These reefs act as natural filters for the water, but the construction of artificial islands has reduced the area of this natural filter and has worsened the quality of the water in the Persian Gulf.

In Bahrain, 182,000 square meters of coral reefs have been lost as a result of frequent dredging of the sands of the seabed near Muharraq Island. Furthermore, 95% of the mangroves in Tubli Bay, which is located in the northeastern area of Bahrain Island, were also found to have been lost due to dredging in land reclamation projects. If the construction of these artificial islands continues, within the next decade, all of the shallow coastal areas will become land, and the offshore areas will become shallower, changing the environment of the Persian Gulf. However, in 2019, an order to ban the extracting and dredging of sand, in a bid to allow the kingdom's seabed to recover from decades of damage, was announced by Bahraini Prime Minister Prince Khalifa bin Salman Al Khalifa.

ポイントは冒頭の Instructions にある通り、できるだけ「自分の言葉」で要約する、つまり問題文からそのまま抜き出すのではなくパラフレーズしてまとめることです。英文自体の語彙レベルが高いので、要約で1級にふさわしい語彙でパラフレーズできる英語力を身につけておくことが求められます。語数制限を破った答案は言語道断です。

英検本番では「内容」「構成」「語彙」「文法」の4つの観点で採点されることが公表されていますが、本書では「内容（構成も含む）」と「文法（語彙も含む）」の解説に焦点をあてるため、「内容点」「文法点」の2つの観点から下記のような本書独自の採点基準を設定しています。

本書での採点基準 （1級）

※この基準は本書独自のもので、公益財団法人 日本英語検定協会が公表しているものではありません。

1. 語数について

90語未満の場合（不足1語につき）	1点減点
90語～110語	減点なし
110語を超える場合（過剰1語につき）	1点減点

2. 文法について

軽度の間違い	大文字・小文字の間違い／句読点の間違い／元の単語が推測できるレベルの綴りの間違い*／冠詞のヌケ・間違い*／名詞の単数・複数の間違い／三単現のsの脱落など	1点減点
重大な間違い	to不定詞か動名詞か／自動詞か他動詞か／時制の不一致／接続詞や前置詞の誤用／不可算名詞、複数形名詞の所有格のような、文法・語法上の誤り／主語または目的語の欠落、あるいは重文・複文の接続詞の脱落のような、構文上の間違い	2～3点減点

※role を roll とするなど意味が変わってしまう綴りのミスは2点減点。※先行詞の前の冠詞のミスは2点減点。※1文中で、ある誤りが2語以上に及ぶ場合でも、明らかにそれが1つの誤りに帰すると思われる場合には1回の減点にとどめるものとする。※someone などの不定代名詞を受ける代名詞に関しては、性差別を避ける観点から、he or she または they とするのが一般的であるが、he / his / him を減点しないものとする。※同じ単語については重複して減点しない。

3. 引用について

- 本文の文を5語以上連続してそのまま引用している場合、その文の内容点は与えないものとする。
- ただし固有名詞あるいはそれに準ずる名詞においては減点しないものとする。

4. 内容について

- 問題文の趣旨を理解していないと思われるものは25点減点とする。
- 採点は減点法とする。具体的な得点は各問題の解説で明示する。
- ただし論理的な整合性に欠ける文（[例] 根拠・理由に結論との整合性がないもの、常識の範囲で理由とは認められないもの）は各2～3点減点する。

解 答 例

Nowadays, many students use online dictionaries, which are easily accessible through their smartphones. Online dictionaries are lightweight, inexpensive, and allow us to listen to the correct pronunciation of words. However, they cannot be used without a Wi-Fi connection. Moreover, students may become too dependent on them, and become too distracted by the smartphone's other functions.

(55 words)

　最近では、多くの学生がスマートフォンから簡単にアクセスできるオンライン辞書を使用している。オンライン辞書は軽量で安価であり、単語の正しい発音を聞くことを可能にする。しかし、Wi-Fi接続がなければ使えない。さらに学生がそうした辞書に依存しすぎたり、スマートフォンのその他の機能に気を取られすぎたりすることがあるかもしれない。

STEP 1
問題文の要点をつかむ

第1段落

　　Students used to use either paper or electronic dictionaries when they studied a foreign language, but nowadays many do not use either option. Instead, they use online dictionaries.

　　学生たちは外国語を勉強するとき、以前は紙の辞書か電子辞書のどちらかを使っていたが、最近はどちらの選択肢も使わない人が多い。代わりにオンライン辞書を使うのだ。

語彙リスト

□	1.	used to (V)	熟	かつて〜していた
□	2.	éither A or B	熟	AかBか
□	3.	nówadàys	副	最近
□	4.	not éither 〜	熟	どちらの〜もない
□	5.	instéad	副	その代わりに
□	6.	ónlíne	形	オンラインの

解説と要旨

　　段落の主張は簡潔に言えば「最近では、多くの学生がオンライン辞書を使用している」です。「外国語を勉強するときに」や「（紙の辞書か電子辞書の）どちらも使わない人が多い」は、そもそも余剰の情報なので、語数制限を考慮すれば省くのが得策です。すべて省かずに書くと、Nowadays, online dictionaries are the most common way to study foreign languages, instead of printed or electronic dictionaries.「現在、外国語を勉強する場合、紙や電子辞書ではなく、オンライン辞書を使うのが最も一般的だ」となります。8点満点で、減点法で採点します。

[**要約例**] Nowadays, many students use online dictionaries.

「最近では、多くの学生がオンライン辞書を使用している」

[**注1**] Nowadays は These days、Today でも可。

[**注2**] 一般論なので複数形 online dictionaries にする。

第2段落

What are the reasons for this? Online dictionaries are most accessible because most students have a smartphone and they can easily access the Internet through it. Online dictionaries are much lighter and cheaper than the other two. Students can listen to the proper pronunciation of words, too.

　この理由は何だろうか。ほとんどの学生がスマートフォンを持っていて、それを用いてインターネットに簡単にアクセスできるので、オンライン辞書へは極めて簡単にアクセスできる。オンライン辞書は、他の2つに比べてはるかに軽量で安価である。学生たちは単語の正しい発音を聞くこともできる。

語彙リスト

☐ **7.**	accéssible	形	アクセスができる、利用できる
☐ **8.**	áccess ～	動	～にアクセスする、利用する
☐ **9.**	much + 比較級	熟	ずっと～
☐ **10.**	próper	形	適切な

解説と要旨

　この段落では、オンライン辞書のメリットが述べられています。それは❶「スマホで簡単にアクセスできる」、❷「軽量である」、❸「安価である」、❹「単語の正しい発音を聞くことができる」の4つです。8点満点で、各区分2点として減点法で採点します。

[**要約例**] They are easily accessible through their smartphones. Online dictionaries are lightweight, inexpensive, and allow us to listen to the correct pronunciation of words.

「それらはスマートフォンで簡単にアクセスできる。軽量で安価であり、単語の正しい発音を聞くことを可能にする」

[**注1**] 「アクセスできる」は accessible とする。available でも可。

[**注2**] through their smartphones は with their smartphones でも可。

[**注3**] 「軽量で」は lightweight とする。lighter でも可。

[**注4**] allow us to listen to ～は help us (to) know ～でも可。

Needless to say, there are some disadvantages to online dictionaries as well. Depending on the Wi-Fi connection, the students may not be able to access them. Most importantly, if the students often use online dictionaries, they will become dependent on them and no longer voluntarily learn new words. They may get distracted by phone calls, emails, videos, and entertainment apps. As a result, they may not be able to focus on studying.

言うまでもなく、オンライン辞書にはいくつかのデメリットもある。Wi-Fi 環境によっては、学生が辞書にアクセスできないこともあるかもしれない。最も重要なのは、学生がオンライン辞書を頻繁に使っていると、それらに依存的になり、自発的に新しい単語を覚えなくなってしまうことだ。電話、E メール、動画、娯楽アプリなどに気を取られるかもしれない。その結果、彼らは勉強に集中できなくなるかもしれない。

語彙リスト

☐ 11.	néedless to say	熟	言うまでもなく
☐ 12.	disadvántage to 〜	熟	〜の不都合な点
☐ 13.	as well	熟	同様に
☐ 14.	Wi-Fi connéction	名	Wi-Fi接続
☐ 15.	most impórtantly	熟	一番重要なことには
☐ 16.	becóme depéndent on 〜	熟	〜に依存する
☐ 17.	no lónger	熟	もはや〜ない
☐ 18.	vòluntárily	副	自発的に
☐ 19.	get distrácted	熟	気が散る、集中できなくなる
☐ 20.	entertáinment app	名	娯楽アプリ
☐ 21.	as a resúlt	熟	その結果
☐ 22.	fócus on 〜	熟	〜に集中する

解説と要旨

　この段落では、オンライン辞書のマイナス面が述べられています。それは❶「Wi-Fi の環境がないと使用できない」、❷「依存しすぎて単語を覚えなくなる」、❸「スマホのその他の機能に気を取られ、勉強に集中できない」。❸の後半部の「勉強に集中できない」は自明なのでなくてもいいでしょう。9点満点で、各区分3点で減点法で採点

します。

[**要約例**] They cannot be used without a Wi-Fi connection. Moreover, students may become too dependent on them, and become too distracted by the smartphone's other functions.

「それらはWi-Fi接続がなければ使えない。さらに、学生がそうした辞書に依存しすぎたり、スマートフォンのその他の機能に気を取られすぎたりすることがあるかもしれない」

[**注1**]「Wi-Fi接続」はa Wi-Fi connection とする。an internet connection でも可。

[**注2**]「集中できない」は「〜の注意をそらす」という意味のdistractを受動態にして、get distracted by the phone's other functions とする。be unable to concentrate on their studies due to other functions でも可。

STEP 2
モニター答案でポイントをつかむ

[**モニター答案例1**][**13 / 25点**]

Many students use online dictionaries because they are much lighter and cheaper than any other dictionary, and students can listen to the proper pronunciation of words. However, they also discourage students from learning new words and ✕ dependent on Wi-Fi condition too much. Moreover, there are

　　　　　　ヌケ→make them too：−2点　　　　　✕ トル：−1点

many elements to prevent students from focusing on studying in it.　　(56 words)

✕ →distractions that：−3点　　　　　　　　　　✕ トル：−1点

[**内容点**] 語数制限を1語オーバーしているので−1点。第1段落はOKです。第2段落は❶がヌケで−2点。第3段落は❶❷はOK。❸は「スマホの他の機能」に対する言及がないので−2点。以上、−5点。

[**文法点**] −7点。「学生が勉強に集中するのを現実に妨げている多くの『阻害要因』」なので、to (V) は不適切。

[**総評**] 英語自体はそれほど悪くないが、内容の漏れが多い。「何となく」まとめるのはやめること。

[モニター答案例2] [0 / 25点]

These days, online dictionaries replace paper or electronic dictionaries among
✗ →Recently, online dictionaries have replaced：－2点
the students. Online dictionaries are very useful and need low cost. But, they also
✗ →トル：－1点　　　　　　　　　　　✗ →cheap：－2点　✗ →However：－1点
have a bad effect for students to impair student's vocabulary skills and your
　　　　✗ →on：－2点　　　　✗ →impairing vocabulary research：－3点　　　✗ →トル：－1点
concentration. It causes that you will decline your grade.　　　　　(46 words)
　　✗ →トル：減点なし

[**内容点**] 第1段落が不十分で－6点。文法点での減点もあります。第2段落は❶❷❹がヌケで－6点。第3段落❶はヌケで－3点。❷は、それらしきことを書いているが表現が適切でないので文法点での減点とする。❸は不十分で－3点。以上、－18点。

[**文法点**] －12点。replace ～は現在形は習慣的行為になり、「～に取って代わった」の意味にはならない。Butの使い方として、But＋カンマ＋SVは不可。最終文は意味不明。

[**総評**] 語法を知らない単語を日本語を頼りに使っているうちは2級レベルではない。

STEP 3
ネイティブスピーカーの答案に学ぶ

模範解答

Recently, online dictionaries have replaced traditional paper or electronic forms as the tool for choice for foreign language study. Reasons for their popularity include instant accessibility, portability and range of functions. However, such dictionaries require internet access to work, and their very universality may lead to overdependence on them or increased distraction from study. (54 words)

近年、外国語学習のツールとして、従来の紙媒体や電子媒体に代わってオンライン辞書が選ばれるようになってきた。その人気の理由は、即座にアクセスできること、持ち運びの利便性、機能が豊富であることなどである。しかし、このような辞書を使うにはインターネットへのアクセスが必要であり、その万能性ゆえに辞書への過度の依存や勉強の妨げになる可能性が増大することがある。

語彙リスト

☐ **1.**	require (O) to (V)	熟	(O) が (V) することを必要とする
☐ **2.**	universálity	名	普遍性、万能性
☐ **3.**	overdepéndence	名	過度の依存
☐ **4.**	distráction	名	気が散ること

N O T E

解 答 例

One advantage of public libraries is that anyone can use them. Although we can access information online, the time spent in libraries offers a unique experience. They also preserve old or invaluable books. However, some downsides are that we have to return books by a certain date and books are sometimes damaged by other borrowers.

(55 words)

公共図書館の利点の1つは、誰でも使えることだ。オンラインで情報は得られるが、図書館で過ごす時間からは独特な経験が得られる。また、図書館は古い本や貴重な本を保存している。しかし、問題点は、本を決まった日までに返さなければならないこと、本が他の借り手によって傷つけられることもあるということだ。

STEP 1
問題文の要点をつかむ

第1段落

One of the greatest things about public libraries is that they are open to all. No special degree or license is required to enter a public library. However, with the rise of technology, the importance of their existence is being questioned.

公共図書館の素晴らしいところの1つは、誰にでも開かれていることだ。公共図書館に入るのに、特別な学位や免許は必要ない。しかし、テクノロジーの台頭により、その存在の重要性が問われている。

語彙リスト

□ **1.**	públic líbrary	名	公共図書館
□ **2.**	be ópen to 〜	熟	〜に開かれている
□ **3.**	degrée	名	学位
□ **4.**	requíre 〜	動	〜を必要とする
□ **5.**	with the rise of 〜	熟	〜の登場とともに
□ **6.**	exístence	名	存在
□ **7.**	be being quéstioned	熟	疑問視されつつある　※受動態の進行形

解説と要旨

第1文「公共図書館の素晴らしいところの1つは、誰にでも開かれていることだ」はこの文の主張で必要です。第2文は第1文の具体化なので必要ありません。8点満点で、減点法で採点します。

[**要約例**] One advantage of public libraries is that anyone can use them.
「公共図書館の利点の1つは、誰でも使えることだ」
[**注1**] One advantage of 〜は One benefit of 〜や One great thing about 〜も可。
[**注2**] anyone can use them は they are accessible to anyone でも可。

第2段落

Why should libraries be saved? The internet certainly provides all the information we need, but the experience we get when we spend time in a library is not one we can get elsewhere. Some libraries are also needed for preserving old books and editions that cannot be found online.

なぜ図書館を維持すべきなのか。インターネットは確かに我々が必要とする情報すべてを提供してくれるが、図書館で時間を過ごすことで我々が得る経験は他では得られないものだ。また、オンラインでは見つからない古い本や版を保存するために必要な図書館もある。

語彙リスト

□ **8.**	save ～	動	～を救う
□ **9.**	cértainly	副	確かに
□ **10.**	províde ～	動	（必要なもの）を与える
□ **11.**	expérience	名	経験
□ **12.**	one	代	この文では an experience を指す
□ **13.**	presérve ～	動	～を保存する
□ **14.**	edítion	名	（本や新聞の）版

解説と要旨

　この段落では公共図書館の存在意義について 2 つ述べられています。❶「図書館で時間を過ごすことで我々が得る経験は、他では得られないものである」、❷「図書館には、（インターネットでは見つからない）古い本や貴重な本が保存されている」です。「インターネットでは見つからない」は語数制限を考えて省いても OK です。9 点満点で、各区分 5 点として減点法で採点します。0 点になった場合、それ以上減点はしません。

[**要約例**] Although we can access information online, the time spent in libraries offers a unique experience. They also preserve old or invaluable books.

「オンラインで情報は得られるが、図書館で過ごす時間からは独特の経験が得られる。また、図書館は古い本や貴重な本を保存している」

[**注1**] we can access information online は、information is readily [easily] available online [on the internet] でも可。

[**注2**] a unique experience は an experience that we cannot get anywhere else でも可。

[注3] invaluable books は precious [very important] books でも可。

第3段落

On the other hand, there are some negative aspects of libraries. When we borrow a book from a library, we must return it within a set period. Furthermore, many people do not feel that they have to return books in perfect condition. Libraries have also seen cases where pages of books are found to be damaged or marked.

　一方、図書館のマイナス面もいくつかある。図書館で本を借りたら、決められた期間内に返さなければならない。しかも、多くの人は本を完璧な状態で返す必要を感じていない。図書館では、本のページが破損していたり、書き込みがされていたりするケースも見られる。

語彙リスト

☐ **15.**	on the other hand	熟	一方
☐ **16.**	négative	形	マイナスの
☐ **17.**	áspect	名	側面
☐ **18.**	bórrow A from B	熟	BからAを（無償で）借りる
☐ **19.**	set	形	一定の
☐ **20.**	fúrthermòre	副	さらに
☐ **21.**	case where SV	熟	SVの場合
☐ **22.**	mark 〜	動	〜に（印など）を記入する

解説と要旨

　ここでは公共図書館のマイナス面が述べられています。❶「返却期日があること」、❷「他の借り手によって傷つけられていることがある」の2つです。8点満点で、各区分4点として減点法で採点します。

[**要約例**] However, some downsides are that we have to return books by a certain date and books are sometimes damaged by other borrowers.

「しかし、問題点は、本を決まった日までに返さなければならないこと、本が他の借り手によって傷つけられることもあるということだ」

[**注1**] return は give 〜 back / give back 〜も可。

[**注2**] we have to return books は library books must be returned でも可。

[注3] 本文の within a set period は by a certain date と言い換えられる。

STEP 2
モニター答案でポイントをつかむ

[モニター答案例1] [3 / 25点]

<u>Someone says</u> that <u>the internet is replacing</u> public libraries. <u>Good point of</u>
✕ → Some people say : −2点　　✕ → there is no need for : −2点　　　　✕ One good thing about : −2点

public libraries is that the time <u>when</u> we spend in a library is irreplaceable and
　　　　　　　　　　　　　　✕ → that : −2点

some libraries have books that <u>can not</u> be found online. However, we must return
　　　　　　　　　　　✕ → cannot : −1点

books which we borrowed within a set period, and moreover, some books are not

✕ perfect condition.　　　　　　　　　　　　　　　　　　　　　　　(57 words)
ヌケ→ returned in : −3点

[内容点] 語数制限を2語オーバーしているので、−2点。第1段落のヌケで−8点。第
2段落は❶❷ともにOK。第3段落は❶はOK。❷は英語として不十分だが、文法点で
の減点とする。以上、−10点。

[文法点] −12点。A replace B ではAとBに対等なものが置かれる。「インターネッ
ト上の図書館」とすれば、まだまし。spend 〜は他動詞なので when はやめて関係代
名詞を用いる。

[総評] 1文1文をしっかり書く必要がある。

[モニター答案例2] [0 / 25点]

We can search information <u>by</u> Internet, so the importance of public libraries
　　　　　　　　　　　　✕ → on the : −2点

<u>existence</u> is being questioned. When we use ✕ <u>internet</u> to get information, it is
✕ → トル : −1点　　　　　　　　　　　　　　ヌケ→ the : −1点

easier than using libraries but some libraries <u>try to preserving</u> old books and
　　　　　　　　　　　　　　　　　　　　✕ → preserve : −2点

editions that <u>can't</u> be found online but library has a lot of negative aspects.
△ →cannot：減点なし

(52 words)

［**内容点**］第1段落の内容のヌケで−8点。第2段落の❶がヌケで−5点。❷はOK。第3段落はnegative aspectsを具体化する必要がある。よって❶❷のヌケとして−8点。以上、−21点。

［**文法点**］−6点。そもそも、try toのうしろは原形不定詞である。

［**総評**］本文をしっかり読んで内容をしっかり理解することが先決。

STEP**3**
ネイティブスピーカーの答案に学ぶ

模 範 解 答

　Public libraries are accessible to all, yet advances in technology have placed their existence under review. Arguments for their continuation include the unique experience of visiting the library, and the role they play in preserving old and rare books. However, borrowing a physical book entails the necessity of returning it, and the possibility of damage.

(55 words)

　公共図書館は誰もが利用できるものだが、テクノロジーの進歩により、その存在は見直されている。その存続を主張する論拠としては、図書館を訪れるというユニークな体験や、古い本や希少な本を保存する役割などがある。しかし、有形の本を借りると返却の必要があり、破損の可能性が伴う。

語 彙 リ ス ト

□ **1.**	pláce 〜 under revíew	熟	〜を見直す
□ **2.**	phýsical book	名	有形の本（＝紙の本）
			※digital bookの対義語
□ **3.**	entáil 〜	動	（必然的に）〜を伴う

解 答 例

A "gap year" is a time off for university students to gain experience outside the classroom. This system allows students to experience other cultures, and gain valuable skills. It also allows for greater motivation, and planning ability. Some universities in Japan have recently introduced this program, and it is hoped that more will follow suit.

(55 words)

「ギャップイヤー」とは、大学生が授業以外の経験を積むための休暇のことである。この制度によって、学生は、異文化を体験したり、貴重なスキルを身につけたりできる。また、意欲や計画能力を高めることも可能になる。日本でも最近、この制度を導入している大学があるが、もっとそうした大学が増えることが望まれる。

STEP 1
問題文の要点をつかむ

第1段落

A "gap year" is a period of time off from formal schooling taken by students to gain experience through activities such as study abroad, internships, and volunteer work before entering university or during university, and occasionally after graduation until starting a job.

「ギャップイヤー」とは、大学入学前や大学在学中、場合によっては卒業してから就職するまでの間、正規の学校教育から離れ、留学やインターンシップ、ボランティアなどの活動を通して経験を積むためのある一定期間の休暇のことである。

語彙リスト

□ 1.	time off	名	休暇
□ 2.	gain 〜	動	〜を得る
□ 3.	ínternship	名	インターンシップ
□ 4.	occásionally	副	時折

解説と要旨

「ギャップイヤー」の説明がなされている文です。「大学入学前や大学在学中、場合によっては卒業後」は語数制限を考えると❶「大学生」で済ますしかないでしょう。while they are still registered at university「大学に籍をおきながら」ともできますが、これでも長いですね。後半の「正規の学校教育から離れ、留学やインターンシップ、ボランティアなどの活動を通して経験を積む」は、❷「授業以外の経験を積む」ぐらいに凝縮します。8点満点で、各区分4点として減点法で採点します。

[**要約例**] A "gap year" is a time off for university students to gain experience outside the classroom.
「『ギャップイヤー』とは、大学生が授業以外の経験を積むための休暇のことである」

[注1] a time off は、2級ならば a holiday（英）や a vacation（米）でも可。

[注2] gain experience の代わりに build up experience あるいは experience の動詞を用いて experience various things とすることもできる。

[注3] outside the classroom は off campus でも可。

第2段落

What can students gain through this experience? A gap year provides the opportunity for students to learn what they could not in the classroom. For instance, they can learn about various cultures and acquire valuable skills. In addition, students who have experienced a gap year have higher motivation and planning ability after entering school compared to students who have not.

この経験を通して、学生は何を得ることができるのだろうか。ギャップイヤーは、教室では学べないことを学ぶ機会を学生に提供する。例えば、さまざまな文化について学び、貴重なスキルを身につけることができる。また、ギャップイヤーを経験した生徒は、体験していない生徒に比べて、入学後の意欲や計画性が高い。

語彙リスト

☐ **5.**	províde A for B	熟	Bに（必要な）Aを与える
☐ **6.**	opportúnity	名	好機
☐ **7.**	acquíre ～	動	～を身につける
☐ **8.**	váluable	形	価値のある
☐ **9.**	skill	名	技術
☐ **10.**	motivátion	名	動機、意欲
☐ **11.**	plánning abílity	名	計画をするための能力、計画性
☐ **12.**	compáred to ～	熟	～と比べて　※受動態の分詞構文

解説と要旨

この段落では「ギャップイヤーの良い所」が述べられています。「教室では学べないことを学べる」ということですが、これは第1段落に書かれているので、それを具体化して❶「さまざまな文化について学び、貴重なスキルを身につけることができる」、さらに❷「意欲や計画能力を高める」まで書いておきましょう。9点満点で、各区分5点として減点法で採点します。0点になった場合、それ以上減点はしません。

［**要約例**］This system allows students to experience other cultures, and gain valuable skills. It also allows for greater motivation, and planning ability.
「この制度によって、学生は、異文化を体験したり、貴重なスキルを身につけたりできる。また、意欲や計画能力を高めることも可能になる」
［**注1**］allow for 〜は「〜を可能にする」という意味の熟語。allow oneself to go for 〜「自らが〜に向かうことを可能にする」からできたと理解しておこう。

第3段落

　In Japan, this system was unfamiliar until now, but now some universities allow this period before and immediately after entering the university to support students. It is hoped that more universities in Japan will become aware of the benefits of this system and adopt it.

　日本ではこの制度はこれまでなじみが薄かったが、現在では大学によっては入学前や入学直後の学生をサポートする期間として認めている。日本のより多くの大学がこの制度の恩恵を認識し、この制度を採用することが望まれる。

語彙リスト

☐ **13.**	ùnfamíliar	形	知られていない
☐ **14.**	immédiately after 〜	熟	〜のすぐ後に
☐ **15.**	becóme awáre of 〜	熟	〜を認識する
☐ **16.**	adópt 〜	動	〜を採用する

解説と要旨

　この段落の前半は❶「日本でもこの制度を導入する大学がある」ということです。後半は、❷「この制度を採用する日本の大学が増えることが望ましい」です。8点満点で、各区分4点として減点法で採点します。
［**要約例**］Some universities in Japan have recently introduced this program, and it is hoped that more will follow suit.
「日本でも最近、このプログラムを導入している大学があるが、もっとそうした大学が増えることが望まれる」
［**注1**］introduce は adopt でも可。
［**注2**］follow suit「例にならう」は adopt this system でも可。

STEP2
モニター答案でポイントをつかむ

[モニター答案例1] [9 / 25点]

A "gap year" enables students to get experience by some activities. They can
✕ →outside the classroom：－3点
improve their skills. Also, they can come to have motivation and planning ability.

In Japan, lately there are some university which enables students to take ✕ gap year.
✕ →nowadays：－2点　　✕ →universities which allow：－2点　　ヌケ→a：－1点
It is hoped that more universities ✕ will introduce this system.　　　(50 words)
ヌケ→in this country：－2点

[**内容点**] 第1段落は❶がヌケで－4点。❷の内容も不適切だが、文法点として減点する。第2段落は❶が不十分なので－2点。❷はOK。第3段落は❶は文法的ミスはあるが、OK。❷はOK。以上、－6点。

[**文法点**] －10点。lately は通例現在完了形か過去形で用いられる。which は先行詞が複数形なら複数の扱いとなる。

[**総評**] 受動態以外でby ～を使うのは、通例「by→交通手段」と覚えておけば、1行目のようなミスは防げる。

[モニター答案例2] [7 / 25点]

Students can gain precious experience in a gap year. They can get an

opportunity to develop valuable skills that can't be learned in the classroom.
▲ →cannot：減点なし
Because of the skills students get higher motivation and planning ability. The
✕ →As a result：－2点　　　　　　　　　　　　　　　　　　✕ →It is hoped that the：－2点
number of universities in Japan which introduce this system is increasing.
✕ →have introduced：－2点　　✕ →will increase：－2点

(48 words)

[**内容点**] 第1段落は❶がヌケで−4点。❷はOK。第2段落は、❶の「さまざまな文化を学ぶ」がヌケで−2点。❷は文法的なミス以外はOK。第3段落の❶はOKだが、❷がないので−4点。以上、−10点。

[**文法点**] −8点。

[**総評**] 日本人の英語には、第3文のような「原因と結果」が不明確なものが多い。常に「原因と結果」を意識すること。

STEP **3**
ネイティブスピーカーの答案に学ぶ

模範解答

　Gap years, which are extending breaks for study during which university students undertake work or study abroad, can provide many advantages, including the gaining of skills, experience and motivation. Gap years have not been common in Japan, but the system is gaining wider acceptance, given the chance for young people to extend and develop themselves.　　　　　　　　　　　　　　　　(55 words)

　ギャップイヤーとは、大学生の就労や留学のための長期休暇のことで、スキルや経験の習得、モチベーションの向上など、多くのメリットを提供しうる。ギャップイヤーは日本では一般的ではなかったが、若者が自己を拡張し、成長させる機会を与えられることから、この制度は広く受け入れられつつある。

語彙リスト

☐ **1.**	Gap years, which ... ,	※ which ... , のカンマに挟まれた部分は「ギャップイヤー」の追加説明になっている。
☐ **2.**	inclúding	前 ～を含めて

解 答 例

Most people do not know exactly what space exploration involves. Its advantages are the improvement of science and technology and the creation of industries and jobs. It could also solve issues such as food shortages and population problems. However, space exploration requires a great deal of time and money without guaranteed results.

(52 words)

ほとんどの人は、宇宙探査がどのようなものかを正確に知らない。その利点は、科学技術の向上、産業や雇用の創出である。また、食糧不足や人口問題などを解決することもできるかもしれない。しかし、宇宙探査は保証される成果なしに莫大な時間とお金を必要とする。

STEP 1
問 題 文 の 要 点 を つ か む

第 1 段 落

Space exploration has long been a worldwide effort to explore the potential of the universe. When many people hear the term "space exploration," they think of rocket launches, space stations, and so on. However, what exactly is being done is probably not well known to most people.

　宇宙探査は昔から、宇宙の可能性を探る世界的な取り組みであった。「宇宙探査」という言葉を聞くと、ロケットの打ち上げや宇宙ステーションなどを思い浮かべる人が多いだろう。しかし、正確にどのようなことが行われているのかは、大半の人におそらくあまり知られていない。

語彙リスト

☐ **1.**	space explorátion	名	宇宙探査
☐ **2.**	wórldwíde	形	世界規模の
☐ **3.**	explóre ～	動	～を探査する
☐ **4.**	poténtial	名	(潜在的な) 可能性
☐ **5.**	the úniverse	名	(天体なども含めた) 宇宙
☐ **6.**	term	名	(一語もしくは複数の語からなる) 言葉、用語
☐ **7.**	rócket launch	名	ロケットの打ち上げ
☐ **8.**	exáctly	副	(疑問詞を修飾して) 正確に

解説と要旨

　この段落では「宇宙探査」に対する、一般的な人の認識が述べられています。筆者の主張は However 以下の「宇宙探査に関して正確にどのようなことが行われているのか大半の人は知らない」です。8点満点で減点法で採点します。

[**要約例**] Most people do not know exactly what space exploration involves.
「ほとんどの人は、宇宙探査がどのようなものかを正確に知らない」

第2段落

What are the advantages of space exploration? First of all, it will contribute to the advancement of scientific knowledge and technology. Finding the origins of the universe will improve not only knowledge but also technology. In addition, it will lead to the creation of industries and jobs. Many people may work in fields we have never dreamed of. Furthermore, working on space development may help solve food shortages, population problems, and other issues.

宇宙探査にはどんなメリットがあるのだろうか。まず最初に、科学の知識や技術の向上に貢献する。宇宙の起源を見つけることは、知識だけでなく技術の向上にもつながる。また、産業や雇用の創出にもつながる。多くの人々が我々が今まで考えたこともない分野で仕事をするかもしれない。さらに、宇宙開発に取り組むことは食糧不足や人口問題などのさまざまな問題の解決にも役立つかもしれない。

語彙リスト

☐ 9.	advántage	名	利点、メリット
☐ 10.	contríbute to ~	熟	~に貢献する
☐ 11.	órigin	名	起源
☐ 12.	in addítion	熟	加えて
☐ 13.	índustry	名	産業
☐ 14.	work on ~	熟	~に取り組む
☐ 15.	help (to) (V)	熟	(V) することに役立つ
☐ 16.	food shórtage	名	食糧不足
☐ 17.	íssue	名	(政治的、社会的な) 問題

解説と要旨

ここでは宇宙探査のプラス面が述べられています。順に、❶「科学技術の進歩」、❷「産業と雇用の創出」、❸「食糧不足や人口問題などの解決」です。9点満点で、各区分3点として、減点法で採点します。

[**要約**] Its advantages are the improvement of science and technology and the creation of industries and jobs. It could also solve issues such as food shortages and population problems.

「その利点は、科学技術の向上、産業や雇用の創出である。また、食糧不足や人口問題などを解決することもできるかもしれない」

[**注1**] the improvement of 〜は、the progress of 〜や advances in 〜でも可。文で書いて it improves 〜も可。

[**注2**] science and technology は and が必要。

[**注3**] the creation of 〜は、文で書いて create 〜あるいは provide us with [give us] 〜とするのも可。

[**注4**] 「(もしかしたら) 〜かもしれない」というニュアンスは could で表す。

[**注5**] such as は前置詞の including で言い換え可。

第3段落

However, there is one big disadvantage of space exploration. Space research involves a long research period, and as a result, it requires a large amount of money. Furthermore, even if huge amounts of public funds are used, the results may not be as expected.

しかし、宇宙探査には１つの大きなデメリットがある。宇宙探査には長い研究期間が必要であり、その結果、多額の資金が必要となる。さらに、巨額の公的資金を投入しても、期待されたような成果が得られないこともあるのだ。

語彙リスト

☐ **18.**	disadvántage	名	不利な点、デメリット
☐ **19.**	invólve 〜	動	〜を必ず伴う、〜が必要である
☐ **20.**	requíre 〜	動	〜を必要とする
☐ **21.**	fúrthermòre	副	さらに
☐ **22.**	fund	名	資金
☐ **23.**	as expécted	熟	期待されたように

解説と要旨

この段落では宇宙探査のマイナス点が２つ述べられています。それぞれ❶「時間と

お金がかかる」、❷「期待された結果が得られないことがある」です。8点満点で、各区分4点として減点法で採点します。

[要約例] However, space exploration requires a great deal of time and money without guaranteed results.

「しかし、宇宙探査は保証される成果なしに莫大な時間とお金を必要とする」

[注1] requires は takes でも可。

[注2] without guaranteed results「保証された結果なしに」は、文で書くなら Good results are not always guaranteed.「よい結果が保証されるとは限らない」、it may not yield [produce] good results「それはよい結果を生み出さないかもしれない」などとすることも可。

STEP2
モニター答案でポイントをつかむ

[モニター答案例1] [15 / 25点]

Most people do not know the true meaning of space exploration. It may be

✗ →improve：－3点

improved scientific knowledge and technology. And it may be able to give us new

industries and new jobs. On the other hand, researching space need a large amount

✗ →requires：－2点

of money and may not provide us with good results.　　　　　　　　(52 words)

[内容点] 第1段落はOK。第2段落は、❶❷はOK だが❸がヌケで－3点。第3段落は❶は、時間に関する言及がないので、－2点。❷はOK。以上、－5点。

[文法点] －5点。need は原則「人」を主語として、require は原則「モノ」を主語にすると覚えておくこと。

[総評] SVOO や SVOC をとらない動詞は be ＋過去分詞 ～の形の受動態はとらない。このミスは多い。

［モニター答案例2］［10 / 25点］

Most people do not know <u>well</u> about most advanced space research. Searching
　　　　　　　　　✗ →much：−1点
the origins of the universe will develop technology and <u>make</u> the creation of
　　　　　　　　　　　　　　　　　　　　　　✗ →lead to：−2点
industries and jobs. Also, space development will help solve many problems. <u>But</u>
　　　　　　　　　　　　　　　　　　　　　　　　　　　　　▲ →However, :減点なし
space research <u>need</u> a large amount of money.　　　　　　　　　(45 words)
　　　✗ →requires：−2点

［**内容点**］第1段落はOK。第2段落は、❶はscienceのヌケで−2点。❷はOK。❸は
「食糧不足」「人口問題」のヌケで−2点。第3段落は❶が不十分で−2点。❷がヌケ
で−4点。以上、−10点。

［**文法点**］−5点。know 〜 wellと言うことはできるが、know＋程度表現＋about 〜
の場合にはwellは使わない。

［**総評**］knowのような基本動詞の使い方がわかっていない人は意外と多い。紙の辞書
でしっかり調べてみるとよい。

STEP 3
ネイティブスピーカーの答案に学ぶ

模範解答

Space exploration, a global endeavor to unravel the universe's mysteries, involves more than rocket launches. While advancing scientific knowledge, stimulating new industries and creating new jobs, it also contributes to solving global issues such as food shortage and population problems. However, the extensive research requires substantial funding, and research outcomes may fall short of expectations.

(55 words)

宇宙の謎を解き明かそうとする世界的な試みである宇宙探査には、ロケット打ち上げ以上のものが含まれる。科学的知識を深め、新たな産業を刺激し、新たな仕事を創出する一方で、食糧不足や人口問題などの地球規模の問題の解決にも貢献する。しかし、そうした広範な研究には多額の資金が必要であり、研究成果が期待を下回る可能性もある。

語彙リスト

□ **1.**	endéavor to (V)	熟	〜する努力
□ **2.**	unrável 〜	動	〜を解明する
□ **3.**	stímulate 〜	動	〜を刺激する

解 答 例

In 2021, fewer young people held a driver's license than other age groups. Reasons for this include the time needed to obtain one, the costs of owning a car, and lack of parking spaces. However, a car often reduces commuting time, especially if you know shortcuts. Also, a license is a handy form of identification.

(55 words)

2021年には、運転免許を持つ若者が他の年齢層に比べて少なかった。この理由は、取得に時間がかかること、車を所有するための費用がかかること、駐車スペースがないことなどが挙げられる。しかし、車があれば、特に近道を知っていれば、通勤時間を短縮できることが多い。また、免許証は身分を証明する便利なものだ。

STEP 1
問題文の要点をつかむ

第1段落

A survey released in 2021 revealed that 51.3% of young adults had a driver's license and 14.4% owned their own car. More than 90% of those between the ages of 35 and 59 had a driver's license, so compared to this group, fewer people in the younger generation had a license.

2021年に発表された調査によると、若年成人の51.3%が運転免許を持ち、14.4%が自家用車を所有していることがわかった。35歳から59歳の人々は9割以上が免許を持っていたので、こうした集団に比べると若い世代は免許を持っている人が少なかった。

語彙リスト

☐ 1.	súrvey	名	（アンケート）調査
☐ 2.	revéal ～	動	～を明らかにする
☐ 3.	more than ～	熟	～を超える
			＊more than ～ は等号を含まないので「～以上の」という訳は厳密には間違いだが、訳においては「～以上」とするのが通例です。less than ～ も同様です。
☐ 4.	compáred to ～	熟	～と比べて　※受動態の分詞構文。
☐ 5.	generátion	名	世代

解説と要旨

「2021年の調査で、運転免許を持っている若者が他の年齢層に比べて少なかった」が主張です。語数制限を考えると、具体的な数字を書く余裕はありません。「今日～」というように一般化したものを可とします。これを8点満点として減点法で採点します。

[要約例] In 2021, fewer young people held a driver's license than other age groups.

「2021年には、運転免許を持つ若者が他の年齢層に比べて少なかった」

[注1] These days[Nowadays]、fewer young people want to drive. などでも可。

第2段落

What are the reasons for this trend? Some people say that it takes a lot of time to obtain a car license. Others say the cost of purchasing and repairing a car is high. Needless to say, finding a parking space is another problem.

　この傾向の理由は何だろうか。自動車免許を取得するのに多くの時間がかかるという人もいる。また、車の購入費や修理費が高いという人もいる。言うまでもなく、駐車スペースの確保も問題だ。

語彙リスト

☐ 6.	trend	名 傾向
☐ 7.	obtáin 〜	動 〜を得る
☐ 8.	púrchase 〜	動 〜を購入する
☐ 9.	repáir 〜	動 〜を修理する
☐ 10.	néedless to say	熟 言うまでもなく

解説と要旨

　この段落では、運転免許をとる若者が減っていることの理由が3つ述べられています。それぞれ、❶「免許取得に時間がかかる」、❷「車の所有にお金がかかる」、❸「駐車スペースを確保しなければならない」ことです。9点満点で、各区分3点として減点法で採点します。

[要約例] Reasons for this include the time needed to obtain one, the costs of owning a car, and lack of parking spaces.

「この理由は、免許の取得に時間がかかること、車を所有するための費用がかかること、駐車スペースがないことなどが挙げられる」

[注1] Reasons for this include 〜は、This is (mainly / largely) due to [because of] 〜とすることも可能。

Certainly, many people may not need a license for their daily commute to work or school. However, with a driver's license and a car, they can often shorten their commute, especially if they know how to avoid busy roads and highways. Another benefit is that a license can be used as a form of identification.

確かに、毎日の通勤や通学に免許は必要ないという人も多いかもしれない。しかし、免許と車があり、特に混雑した道路や幹線道路を避ける方法を知っていれば、通勤時間を短縮できることが多いかもしれない。もう1つの利点は、免許証が一種の身分証明書として使えることだ。

語彙リスト

☐ **11.**	cértainly	副	確かに
☐ **12.**	commúte	名	通勤、通学（距離、時間）
☐ **13.**	shórten ~	動	~を短くする
☐ **14.**	avóid ~	動	~を避ける
☐ **15.**	búsy	形	人（車）が多い
☐ **16.**	híghway	名	幹線道路　※高速道路ではない
☐ **17.**	bénefit	名	恩恵
☐ **18.**	a form of ~	熟	~の一形態
☐ **19.**	identificátion	名	身分証明書

解説と要旨

ここでは、運転免許をとる利点が2つ述べられています。それぞれ❶「特に混まない道路を知っていれば通勤時間を短縮できる」、❷「免許証は身分を証明するのに便利だ」です。❶の「特に混まない道路を知っていれば」はなくても減点しないものとします。8点満点で、各区分4点として減点法で採点します。

[**要約例**] However, a car often reduces commuting time, especially if you know shortcuts. Also, a license is a handy form of identification.

「しかし、車があれば、特に近道を知っていれば、通勤時間を短縮できることが多い。また、免許証は身分を証明する便利なものだ」

[**注1**] know shortcuts は know the roads well でも可。

[**注2**] a handy form of は an alternative form of としても可。

STEP 2
モニター答案でポイントをつかむ

[モニター答案例1] [22 / 25点]

Fewer young adults have driver's licenses or their own cars because it is

difficult to obtain licenses or <u>hold</u> cars in terms of time, costs or ✕ spaces.
✕ →own：ー2点   ヌケ→parking：ー1点

However, they can be useful to shorten commuting time or to show who they are,

so there are both good and bad points.   (50 words)

[内容点] 第1段落はOK。第2段落は、❶❷❸すべてOK。第3段落は、❶❷ともに
OK。以上、減点なし。素晴らしい。
[文法点] ー3点。hold は「～を手に持つ」イメージ。
[総評] 最後の一文 (there are both ...) は、英語的には「漠然から具体の流れ」を意識
して文頭に置くべきである。

[モニター答案例2] [11 / 25点]

These days, the number of young people who have a ✕ license is decreasing.
ヌケ→driver's：ー1点

This is because it is hard for them to obtain a car license and find a parking space.

On the other hand, when they have a driver's license and a car, they can get a lot of

benefits.   (51 words)

[内容点] 第1段落はOKだが、語数を取り過ぎ。第2段落は❶は不十分で、ー2点、❷
のヌケでー3点。❸はOK。第3段落は、❶❷のヌケでー8点。以上、ー13点。
[文法点] ー1点。

[**総評**] 文法的なミスがないのは素晴らしい。あとは内容吟味をしっかりとやること。

STEP3
ネイティブスピーカーの答案に学ぶ

05

模範解答

　In 2021, only a little over half of young people held a driver's license, compared with over 90% of people aged between 35 and 59. This discrepancy may be due to perceived time and financial commitments involved, or a dearth of parking options. However, commuting by car can save time, and licenses make practical IDs.　　　　(55 words)

　2021年には、35歳から59歳の90%以上が運転免許を取得しているのに対し、若者の運転免許保有率は半数強に過ぎなかった。この違いは、時間的・金銭的な負担が大きいとみなされていることや、駐車場の不足が原因かもしれない。しかし、車通勤は時間の節約になるし、免許証は実用的な身分証明書になる。

語彙リスト

□ **1.**	discrépancy	名	相違
□ **2.**	fináncial	形	財政に関わる
□ **3.**	commítment	名	(通例s) 義務、責任
□ **4.**	dearth	名	欠乏
□ **5.**	práctical	形	実用的な

解答例

Almost half of Japanese university students live by themselves. The main advantage of doing so is that you can live a life of freedom without interference from anyone else. However, one downside is that you are solely responsible for doing housework. Also, not having anyone to talk to may make you feel lonely.

(53 words)

日本の大学生の半数近くが一人暮らしをしている。その大きなメリットは、他の誰かに干渉されず、自由な生活ができることだ。しかし、デメリットとしては、家事をする責任を自分一人で負うことだ。また、話し相手がいなくて寂しい思いをすることもある。

STEP 1
問題文の要点をつかむ

第1段落

According to a recent survey of Japanese university students, more than 40% of them either rent a house or apartment. It seems that many students, although less than half, live alone after entering university.

日本人大学生を対象とした最近の調査によると、その4割以上が一戸建てかアパートを借りている。半数以下とはいえ、大学入学時から一人暮らしをしている学生が多いようだ。

語彙リスト

□ 1.	súrvey	名	(アンケート) 調査
□ 2.	rent ～	動	(お金を出して) ～を借りる
□ 3.	although less than half	※後に続く自明のof them が省略されている。	

解説と要旨

ここでは「4割以上の日本人大学生が一人暮らしをしている」が主張です。この主張を要約に入れるべきでしょう。8点満点で、減点法で採点します。主語の「4割以上の日本人大学生」は「半数近くの日本人大学生」とするのが望ましいですが、「多くの大学生」としても許容されるかもしれません。

[**要約例**] Almost half of Japanese university students live by themselves.
「日本の大学生の半数近くが一人暮らしをしている」
[**注1**] live by themselves は live on their own でも可。

第 2 段 落

What are the advantages of living alone? The greatest advantage is that you can live freely without anyone interfering in your life. You do not have to adjust to your family's lifestyle or worry about what time you will be home. Even on holidays, nobody wakes you up, so you may sleep longer.

　一人暮らしのメリットは何だろうか。一番のメリットは、誰にも干渉されずに自由に生活できることだ。家族の生活スタイルに合わせる必要もないし、帰宅時間を気にする必要もない。休みの日でも誰にも起こされないので、ゆっくり眠れるかもしれない。

語彙リスト

□ **4.**	without anyone (V)ing	熟	誰かに (v) されることなく ※ anyone は動名詞 (V) の意味上の主語の働き。
□ **5.**	interfére in ～	熟	～に干渉する
□ **6.**	adjúst to ～	熟	～に合わせる
□ **7.**	wake ～ up / up ～	熟	～の目を覚まさせる、～を起こす

解説と要旨

　ここでは「一人暮らしの良い面」が述べられています。第2文「一番のメリットは、誰にも干渉されずに自由に生活できることだ」が主張で、第3文以降はその具体化なので、第2文だけで十分です。❶「誰にも干渉されず」、❷「自由に生活できる」がポイントです。8点満点で各区分4点として減点法で採点します。

[**要約例**] The main advantage of doing so is that you can live a life of freedom without interference from anyone else.

「その大きなメリットは、他の誰かに干渉されず、自由な生活ができることだ」

[**注1**] live a life of freedom は live the way you want to、live as you like でも可。

[**注2**] without interference from anyone else は、視点を変えて without considering other people's lifestyles「他の人の生活スタイルに気を使うことなく」としてもよい。

第3段落

However, there are some disadvantages. One of them is that you will need to do all the housework by yourself. Doing housework surely improves your life skills, but it can be stressful because nobody helps you with it. Also, when you go home, there is no one to talk to, so you may feel lonely.

しかし、いくつかのデメリットもある。その1つは、家事をすべて自分でやらなければならないことだ。家事をすることで生活力がつくのは確かだが、誰も手伝ってくれないのでストレスになりうる。また、家に帰っても話し相手がいないので、寂しい思いをするかもしれない。

語彙リスト

☐ **8.**	by onesélf	熟	ただ1人で、独力で
☐ **9.**	súrely	副	確かに
☐ **10.**	impróve ～	動	～を改善する
☐ **11.**	life skill	名	生活力、生きていく技術
☐ **12.**	stréssful	形	ストレスの多い

解説と要旨

　この段落では「一人暮らしの悪い面」が2つ述べられています。それは❶「家事を1人でやらなければならない」、❷「話し相手がいないので寂しい」です。9点満点で、各区分5点として減点法で採点します。0点になった場合、それ以上減点はしません。

[**要約例**] However, one downside is that you are solely responsible for doing housework. Also, not having anyone to talk to may make you feel lonely.

「しかし、デメリットとしては、家事をする責任を自分一人で負うことだ。また、話し相手がいなくて寂しい思いをすることもある」

[**注1**]「デメリット」はdownsideとする。

[**注2**] you are solely responsible for doing houseworkは、all household chores have to be done aloneやno one helps you with your houseworkなども可。

[**注3**] 後半はyou may feel lonely when you have no one to talk toでも可。

[**注4**] talk toはtalk withでも可。

STEP **2**
モニター答案でポイントをつかむ

[モニター答案例 1] [20 / 25点]

Many Japanese university students live alone. Living alone has some

advantages. You can live on your own pace and no one interrupts your plan.
                    ✕ →at：−2点

However, if you live alone, no one helps you with your housework. Furthermore,

you may want someone whom ✕ can talk with.   (45 words)
                 ヌケ→you：−3点

[**内容点**] 第1段落はOK。第2段落は、文法ミスはあるが❶❷ともにOK。第3段落は、
❶❷ともにOK。以上、減点なし。
[**文法点**] −5点
[**総評**] live alone が3回も出てきている。同じ語句の反復はできるだけ避けるのが英
語流ということを覚えておきたい。

[モニター答案例 2] [14 / 25点]

Many Japanese students have been living alone since entering university.

Living alone is good ✕ that you need not care about person who you live with. But
           ヌケ→in：−2点   ✕ →people：−2点   ▲ →However,：減点なし
you have to do all housework by yourself. Also, there are nobody to talk ✕ and you
                           ✕ →is：−1点   ヌケ→with：−2点
may feel lonely.   (45 words)

[**内容点**] 第1段落はOK。第2段落は❶はOKだが、❷がヌケで−4点。第3段落は、
❶❷ともにOK。以上、−4点。
[**文法点**] −7点。in that SV で「SV という点において」の意味。a person「1人の

人」に対して people「2人以上の人々」。there is/are ～.「～がある」は～の数で is
か are が決まる。

[**総評**] 内容面はよくできているが、基本的文法ミスが多いのが残念。

STEP **3**
ネイティブスピーカーの答案に学ぶ

06

模範解答

　A little under half of all university students in Japan choose to live by
themselves in a rented accommodation. There are notable advantages to
this, such as independence and the freedom to schedule your lifestyle on
your own terms, though potential loneliness and the burden of having to
do housework alone can be downsides. (54 words)

日本の大学生の半数弱が賃貸住宅での一人暮らしを選んでいる。これには、独立性や、自分の
生活スタイルに合わせてスケジュールを立てられる自由などの素晴らしい利点があるが、孤独になり
やすいことや、家事を一人でこなさなければならない負担はデメリットとなりうる。

語彙リスト

☐ **1.**	accommodátion	图	居住施設
☐ **2.**	nótable	形	目立った
☐ **3.**	indepéndence	图	独立
☐ **4.**	on one's own terms	熟	自分自身の条件に基づいて
☐ **5.**	búrden	图	重荷

解答例

Japanese high school students use social media more than other age groups. It provides them with ways to interact with others and easy access to information. However, information on it is not always correct, overuse can cause depression and other mental illnesses, and postings can be read by anyone, putting the user at risk.

(54 words)

日本の高校生は他の年齢層よりもソーシャルメディアを多く利用している。それは、他者と交流し、情報に簡単にアクセスする方法を彼らに提供する。しかし、そこにある情報は必ずしも正しいものではなく、過剰な利用はうつなどの精神疾患を引き起こす可能性があり、また、投稿は誰でも読むことができるので、利用者が危険にさらされることもある。

STEP 1
問題文の要点をつかむ

第1段落

In Japan, while more than 90% of all age groups use social networking sites, the highest rate of social media use was among high school students. Of all these sites, messaging apps are the most widely used by them.

日本では全年齢層の90%以上がSNSを利用しているが、ソーシャル・ネットワーキング・サイトの利用率が最も高かったのは高校生だった。そのようなサイトの中でもメッセージアプリが高校生に最も広く利用されている。

語彙リスト

□ **1.**	age group	名	年齢層
□ **2.**	rate	名	率
□ **3.**	méssaging app	名	メッセージアプリ
			※ app は application program [software] の略

解説と要旨

この段落では、❶「他の年齢層より高校生が」、❷「ソーシャルメディアを利用している」が主題です。後半の記述との関係や語数制限から「特にメッセージアプリを多く利用している」はなくてもよいでしょう。8点満点で、各区分4点として減点法で採点します。

[**要約例**] Japanese high school students use social media, especially messaging apps, more than other age groups.

「日本の高校生は他の年齢層よりもソーシャルメディア、特にメッセージアプリを多く利用している」

[**注1**] 前ページの[解答例]では especially messaging apps は語数の関係で省いている。

[注3] 「SNS」は英語では social media と表記するのが一般的。

第2段落

　　Why do so many people use social media? The biggest advantage of it is that it provides them with many ways to connect with others. Also, they can get the information they want to get in a short time, which is very convenient.

　　なぜそれほど多くの人がソーシャルメディアを利用するのか。その最大の利点は、他人とつながるための多くの方法を提供してくれることだ。また、得たい情報を短時間で得ることができ、とても便利だ。

語彙リスト

☐			
☐	**4.**	províde A with B	熟 A に B を与える
☐	**5.**	connéct with ～	熟 ～とつながる
☐	**6.**	in a short time	熟 短時間で（動作が完了する）

解説と要旨

　　この段落では人々がソーシャルメディアを利用している理由が2つ述べられています。それは❶「他者とつながること」、❷「情報に簡単にアクセスできること」です。8点満点で、各区分4点として減点法で採点します。

[要約例] It provides them with ways to interact with others and easy access to information.

「それ（ソーシャルメディア）は、他者と交流し、情報に簡単にアクセスする方法を彼らに提供する」

[注1] interact with others は communicate with others、get in touch with others、contact others でも可。contact は他動詞であることに注意。

[注2] easy access to information は、文として書くなら information is easily [readily] available [accessible] となる。

Despite these advantages, you have to be careful because not all information on social media is correct. Some of it may be false information. Furthermore, using social media can cause anxiety, depression, and other health problems. Finally, since anyone can read social media posts, posting personal information, such as where you live or when you will be away from home, can put you at risk.

このような利点はあるものの、ソーシャルメディア上のすべての情報が正しいとは限らないので、注意しなければならない。中には嘘の情報もあるかもしれない。さらに、ソーシャルメディアの利用は、不安やうつ、その他の健康問題を引き起こす可能性がある。最後に、ソーシャルメディア上の投稿は誰でも読むことができるので、どこに住んでいるか、いつ家を空けるのかといった個人情報を投稿すると、自身に危険が降りかかる可能性がある。

語彙リスト

☐ 7.	despíte ~	前 ~にもかかわらず
☐ 8.	false	形 嘘の
☐ 9.	fúrthermòre	副 さらに
☐ 10.	anxíety	名 不安
☐ 11.	depréssion	名 うつ
☐ 12.	since ~	接 ~なので　※読者も知っていると想定される常識的理由を示す。
☐ 13.	post	名 投稿　※発音は /poust/ で動詞も同形。
☐ 14.	put ~ at risk	熟 ~を危険にさらす

解説と要旨

この段落ではソーシャルメディアのマイナス面が3つ述べられています。それは❶「ソーシャルメディア上の情報は必ずしも正しいとは限らない」、❷「ソーシャルメディアの利用はうつなどの精神疾患を引き起こす可能性がある」、(「うつ」はなくてもOK)、❸「投稿は誰でも読むことができるので、投稿者を危険にさらすかもしれない」。9点満点で各区分3点として減点法で採点します。

[要約例] Information on it is not always correct, overuse can cause depression and other mental illnesses, and postings can be read by anyone, putting the user at risk.

「ソーシャルメディア上の情報は必ずしも正しいものではなく、過剰な利用はうつなどの精神疾患を引き起こす可能性があり、また、投稿は誰でも読むことができるので、利用者が危険にさらされることもある」

［注1］ 第1文 は social media can give you false information と か、you cannot always rely on information on social media などと書くこともできる。

［注2］ cause depression and other mental illnesses は、簡単に書けば make its users mentally ill となる。

［注3］ posting も「投稿」を指して使える。最終文は Posting personal information online increases the likelihood of being involved in crime.「ネット上への個人情報の投稿は犯罪に巻き込まれる可能性を高める」などと書くこともできる。

STEP2
モニター答案でポイントをつかむ

［モニター答案例1］［21 / 25点］

　　Most people, regardless of their age, are now using social media because it enables them to contact others in multiple ways and to gain information quickly. However, people must be cautious in using these tools because they sometimes give people false information. Moreover, using social media could lead to various health problems and risk the users' privacy.　　　　　　　　　(57 words)

［**内容点**］語数制限を2語オーバーしているので−2点。第1段落は❶が不十分で−2点。❷はOK。第2段落は、❶❷ともにOK。第3段落は❶❷❸ともにOK。以上、−4点。

［**文法点**］ミスはない。素晴らしい。

［**総評**］英文、使用語彙もレベルが高くて、準1級を目指せるレベルだ。

Social media is widely spread in most age groups, especially in high school

✕ →used：-2点　　　　　　　　　　　　　✕ →by：-2点

students. This is because they can connect with others and get information

quickly. However, it may provide them with false information and cause health

▲ →give them：減点なし

problems. It might be dangerous to post private information.　　(46 words)

07

［**内容点**］第1段落は❶❷ともにOK。第2段落は、❶❷ともにOK。第3段落は、❶❷はOKだが、❸は「投稿は誰でも読める」のヌケで-3点。以上、-3点。

［**文法点**］-4点。provide A with Bは「主にプラスのものを提供する」の意味なので、ここでは不適切。spreadは「（うわさ、細菌、思想などが）広がる」の意味。このレベルの単語を使用する際には、十分な注意が必要。

［**総評**］全体的に出来はよいが、用法をあまり知らない少し難しめの単語はその使用を避けるべき。

STEP **3**
ネイティブスピーカーの答案に学ぶ

Social networking is common among all age groups, but is especially popular with high schoolers. Messaging sites offer people a variety of ways to interact, as well as instant access to information. However, the veracity of such information is debatable, and privacy concerns are an ongoing issue, so such services should be used with caution.　(55 words)

ソーシャル・ネットワーキングはあらゆる年齢層に普及しているが、特に高校生に人気がある。メッセージング・サイトは、人々が交流するためのさまざまな方法を提供するだけでなく、情報に即座にアクセスすることを可能にする。しかし、そのような情報の信ぴょう性には議論の余地があり、プライバシーへの懸念は現在進行中の問題であるため、このようなサービスの利用には注意が必要である。

語彙リスト

☐ **1.**	a varíety of ～	熟	さまざまな～
☐ **2.**	interáct	動	交流する
☐ **3.**	verácity	名	信ぴょう性
☐ **4.**	debátable	形	議論の余地がある
☐ **5.**	concérn	名	懸念
☐ **6.**	óngòing	形	現在進行中の

N O T E

解答例

Nowadays, taking notes on computers is more common than writing on paper, but research suggests the latter is better for the brain. When writing by hand, you remain focused and remember information more easily. However, paper memos are easily lost, and they are relatively hard to share with others. Also, your handwriting might be unreadable.

(55 words)

　現在では、コンピューターを使ってメモを取る方が紙に書くよりも一般的だが、後者の方が脳に良いということを研究が示唆している。手で書く時は集中力が持続し、情報を記憶しやすくなる。しかし、紙のメモは容易に紛失し、他人と共有するのは比較的難しい。また、手書きの字は読みにくいかもしれない。

STEP 1
問 題 文 の 要 点 を つ か む

第1段落

Nowadays, when taking notes, more people use computers than write by hand. However, according to a research team from a university in Norway, the brain was more active when subjects wrote by hand than when they typed on a keyboard.

　現在では、メモを取るとき、手書きよりもコンピューターを使う人が多い。しかし、ノルウェーの大学の研究チームによると、被験者がキーボードでタイプした時よりも、手書きした時の方が脳が活性化したという。

語彙リスト

□ 1.	take a note	熟	メモ（ノート）を取る
□ 2.	write by hand	熟	手で書く
□ 3.	áctive	形	活発な
□ 4.	súbject	名	被験者
□ 5.	type	動	タイプで打つ

解説と要旨

　前半の主張は❶「現在では、紙に書くよりもコンピューターを使ってメモを取る方が一般的である」です。後半の主張は、❷「手書きの方が脳が活性化する」です。8点満点で、各区分4点として、減点法で採点します。

[要約例] Nowadays, taking notes on computers is more common than writing on paper, but research suggests the latter is better for the brain.

「現在では、コンピューターを使ってメモを取る方が紙に書くよりも一般的だが、後者の方が脳に良いということを研究が示唆している」

[注1] nowadays は these days や today でも可だが、recently は通例現在完了や過去で使われるので避ける。

[**注2**]「メモをとる」は一般論なのでnoteを複数形にする。

[**注3**] on computersはusing computersでも可。

[**注4**] popular「人気がある」はcommon「普及している」とは異なるが可。

[**注5**] research「研究」は通例不可算名詞として使われる。

[**注6**]「〜を示唆する」はsuggests 〜とする。indicatesやshowsでも可。

[**注7**]「後者」はthe latterとする。

第2段落

What are the advantages of writing by hand? One advantage of it is that taking notes with paper and pen is very useful when studying. It may not be as fast as typing on a computer, but you stay focused while writing notes by hand. Also, the information is easier to remember because your fingers are not moving on their own without thinking as they do when you type.

手書きの利点は何だろうか。その利点の1つは紙とペンを使ってメモを取るのは、勉強の際に非常に役に立つということである。手で書くのは、コンピューターでのタイピングほど速くはないかもしれないが、手書きでメモを書いている間は集中力が持続する。また、タイピングの時のように何も考えずに指が勝手に動くわけではないので、情報が記憶に残りやすい。

語彙リスト

□	6.	stay fócused	熟 集中力が持続する
□	7.	on one's own	熟 独力で、自分勝手に

解説と要旨

この段落では「手書きで書くことのプラス面」が2つ書かれています。それは❶「集中力が持続する」、❷「情報を記憶しやすくなる」です。8点満点で、各区分4点として減点法で採点します。

[**要約例**] When writing by hand, you remain focused and remember information more easily.

「手で書く時は集中力が持続し、情報を記憶しやすくなる」

[**注1**] remain 〜は「〜のままである」という意味。Writing by hand keeps you focused and makes it easier to retain information in your mind.「手で書くことによって集中力が持続して情報が頭に残りやすくなる」と書くこともできる。

［**注2**］information は不可算名詞なので s をつけないように注意。

第3段落

However, handwriting also has some disadvantages. One of the problems is that paper memos are easy to lose. Another one is that memos are difficult to share with others. It is also possible that your handwriting is so poor that nobody else can read it.

08

しかし、手書きにはいくつかのデメリットもある。そうした問題の1つは、紙のメモは紛失しやすいことだ。もう1つは、メモを他の人と共有するのが難しいことだ。また、字があまりに下手で、他の誰にも読んでもらえないということもあり得る。

語彙リスト

□ **8.**	hándwriting	名	手書き、筆跡
□ **9.**	share A with B	熟	A を B と共有する
□ **10.**	it is póssible that SV	熟	SV ということが起こりうる

解説と要旨

この段落では「手書きで書くことのマイナス面」が3つ書かれています。それは❶「容易に紛失すること」、❷「人と共有するのが難しいこと」、❸「読みにくいかもしれないこと」です。9点満点で、各区分3点として、減点法で採点します。

［**要約例**］However, paper memos are easily lost, and they are relatively hard to share with others. Also, your handwriting might be unreadable.

「しかし、紙のメモは容易に紛失し、他人と共有するのは比較的難しい。また、手書きの字は読みにくいかもしれない」

［**注1**］最終文は語数が許せば your handwriting might be difficult for others to read とすることも可能。

［**注2**］unreadable は、やや難しいが illegible「判読不可能な」でも可。

STEP 2
モニター答案でポイントをつかむ

[モニター答案例1] [16 / 25点]

　　These days, the number of people using computers instead of writing by hand when taking notes is increasing but in fact the brain works more actively and you can stay more focused and remember information more easily when writing by hand. However, it is disadvantageous to lose memos easily and be unable to share
　　　　　　　　　　　　　　　　　　✗ →because you can：−2点　　　　　　　　✗ →cannot：−2点
them with others.
　　　　　　　　　　　　　　　　　　　　　　　　　　　　　　　(57 words)

[内容点] 語数制限を2語オーバーしているので−2点。第1段落は❶❷ともにOK。第2段落は、❶❷ともにOK。第3段落は❶❷はOKだが、❸のヌケで−3点。以上、−5点。
[文法点] −4点。最終文は、to不定詞を用いると仮定の話になってしまうので、because〜を用いて現実の話へと変換しなければならない。
[総評] よくできている。次は準1級に挑戦！

[モニター答案例2] [0 / 25点]

　　Writing note with your hand has both advantages and disadvantages. One
　　　　　　✗ →notes：−1点　✗ hands：−1点
advantages of it is that you can keep focused on your writings.
✗ →advantage：−1点　　　　　　　　　　　　　　　　✗ →writing：−1点
One of other advantages is that you can remember information easily. However,
✗ →Another advantage：−2点
one disadvantage is that paper writings are easy to loss. Moreover, one of other
　　　　　　　　　　　　✗ →paper is easy to lose：−4点　　　　✗ →Another disadvantage：−2点
disadvantages is that theses are difficult to share with others.　　(59 words)
　　　　　　　　　✗ →paper is：−2点

[**内容点**] 語数制限を4語オーバーしているので−4点。第1段落は**❶**がヌケで−4点。**❷**は不十分で−2点。第2段落は**❶❷**ともにOK。第3段落は、**❶**は文法ミスがあるものの内容はOK、**❷**はOK。**❸**はヌケで−3点。以上、−13点。

[**文法点**] −14点。loss「失うこと」は名詞、lose 〜「〜を失う」とは区別すること。また、advantage / disadvantage の用法を学習しておくこと。

[**総評**] 名詞を使う時は、「単数か複数か」をしっかり考える癖をつけること。

STEP 3
ネイティブスピーカーの答案に学ぶ

模範解答

It has been scientifically proven that taking notes by hand results in better cognition than when using a keyboard. Due to the physiological processes involved, written notes offer the advantage of greater focus and higher retention of material. Written notes have their drawbacks, however; they are easy to lose and sometimes illegible to others.

(54 words)

手書きでノートを取る方が、キーボードを使うよりも認知力が高まることは科学的に証明されている。生理的なプロセスが関係するため、筆記メモは集中力が高まり、内容をより定着させることができるという利点がある。しかし、手書きのメモには欠点もある。紛失しやすく、時には他の人が読めないこともある。

語彙リスト

□ **1.**	resúlt in 〜	熟	〜の結果をもたらす
□ **2.**	cognítion	名	認知
□ **3.**	physiológical	形	生理的な
□ **4.**	reténtion	名	保持
□ **5.**	dráwback	名	欠点
□ **6.**	illégible	形	(文字が) 判読しづらい

解答例

It is said that machine translation has become more accurate and will be more widely used, even in the business world. It has the advantages of being economical in terms of time and cost. However, it has difficulty understanding the unwritten cultural backgrounds of different countries, so its translations may be incorrect.

(52 words)

機械翻訳の精度が向上しており、ビジネスの世界でさえ、その普及が進むだろうと言われている。機械翻訳は時間とコストの観点で経済的であるという利点がある。しかし、それはさまざまな国の書かれていない文化的背景を理解することが困難なため、翻訳に誤りが生じるかもしれない。

STEP 1
問題文の要点をつかむ

第1段落

Machine translation, which uses computers to perform translation, is said to have improved in accuracy in recent years. And it is expected that machine translation will be used by more companies. Machine translation itself has existed for some time. However, the results were not very accurate and were not suitable for serious business use.

コンピューターを使って翻訳を行う機械翻訳は、近年その精度が向上したと言われている。そして、今後さらに多くの企業で機械翻訳が使われるようになると予想されている。機械翻訳自体はしばらく前から存在していた。しかし、その結果はあまり正確ではなく、本格的なビジネス利用には適していなかった。

語彙リスト

☐ **1.**	machíne translátion	名	機械翻訳
☐ **2.**	impróve in áccuracy	熟	正確さの点で向上する
☐ **3.**	machíne translátion itsélf	熟	機械翻訳そのもの ※itselfは主語と同格の関係にあり、主語を強調する働き。
☐ **4.**	exíst	動	存在する
☐ **5.**	suítable (for ~)	形	(~に) 適している

解説と要旨

第1～2文が本文の主張なので、ここを❶「機械翻訳の精度が向上した」、❷「(ビジネスの世界でも) 普及が進むと言われている」とまとめます。「ビジネスの世界でも」はなくても可とします。さらに、第2段落以降を読むと、第3～4文は特に重要な情報ではないので省くことにします。8点満点で、各区分4点として減点法で採点します。

[要約例] It is said that machine translation has become more accurate and will be more widely used, even in the business world.

「機械翻訳の精度が向上しており、ビジネスの世界でさえ、その普及が進むだろうと言われている」

[注1] S is said to (V). から It is said that SV. への書き換えは定石。

[注2] accurate は「正確な」という意味。前半は the accuracy of machine translation has improved でも可。

[注3] 後半は will be more common でも可。

第2段落

How will machine translation benefit businesses and language learning? The biggest advantage is the short time required for translation. With machine translation, a simple document can be translated in a few seconds. This allows you to finish the task in a shorter time. This also means that you can lower translation costs.

機械翻訳はビジネスや言語学習にどのようなメリットをもたらすのだろうか。最大の利点は、翻訳に要する時間が短いことだ。機械翻訳を使えば、簡単な文書なら数秒で翻訳できる。そのため、より短い時間で作業を終えることができる。これは、翻訳コストを下げることができるということでもある。

語彙リスト

☐ 6.	bénefit ~	動	~に恩恵を与える
☐ 7.	dócument	名	文書
☐ 8.	in a few séconds	熟	数秒で
☐ 9.	allów (O) to (V)	熟	(O) が (V) するのを可能にする
☐ 10.	lower ~	動	~を下げる

解説と要旨

この段落では、機械翻訳のプラス面が2つ述べられています。それは❶「翻訳に要する時間が短い」、❷「翻訳にかかるコストが安い」です。9点満点で、❶は4点、❷は5点として減点法で採点します。

[要約例] It has the advantages of being economical in terms of time and cost.

「機械翻訳は時間とコストの観点で経済的であるという利点がある」

[注1] 書き出しは Its main advantages are 〜 などでも可。

第3段落

On the other hand, there are also some problems. Communication often involves cultural backgrounds that do not necessarily appear in the texts themselves. Unlike human translators, machines lack awareness of the unstated cultural assumptions that communication between countries requires, so the translations can be wrong.

　一方、いくつかの問題もある。意思の疎通には、テクストそのものには必ずしも現れない文化的背景が含まれることが多い。人間の翻訳者とは異なり、機械は国と国との意思の疎通に必要となる暗黙の文化的前提に対する意識が欠けているため、翻訳が誤ってしまうことがあるのだ。

語彙リスト

□ **11.**	on the other hand	熟	一方
□ **12.**	invólve 〜	動	〜を必ず伴う
□ **13.**	cúltural báckground	名	文化的背景
□ **14.**	not nècessárily	熟	必ずしも〜ない
□ **15.**	unlíke 〜	前	〜と違って
□ **16.**	awáreness	名	意識
□ **17.**	unstáted	形	述べられていない
□ **18.**	requíre 〜	動	〜を必要とする

解説と要旨

　ここでは機械翻訳のマイナス面が2つ述べられています。それらは❶「国と国との意思の疎通に必要な文化的な背景の理解が困難」、❷「翻訳に誤りが生じる可能性」です。8点満点で、各区分4点として減点法で採点します。

[**要約例**] However, it has difficulty understanding the unwritten cultural backgrounds of different countries, so its translations may be incorrect.

　「しかし、それはさまざまな国の書かれていない文化的背景を理解することが困難なため、翻訳に誤りが生じるかもしれない」

[**注1**]　前半は It is difficult for machine translation to capture the unwritten cultural background of various countries. と書くこともできる。

STEP 2
モニター答案でポイントをつかむ

[モニター答案例1] [18 / 25点]

Translation using computers has become ✕ accurate and suited for business
　　　　　　　　　　　　　　　　　ヌケ→more：－1点

use, so it will be used by more companies. Machine translation takes ✕ shorter
　　　　　　　　　　　　　　　　　　　　　　　　　　　　　　　ヌケ→a：－1点

time and costs less, which is good for business and language learning. However, it

is difficult for machine translation to understand cultural background.　(46 words)
　　　　　　　　　　　　　　　　　　　　　　　✕ →backgrounds：－1点

[内容点] 第1段落は❶❷ともにOK。第2段落は、❶❷ともにOK。第3段落は❶は
OK。❷はヌケで－4点。以上、－4点。
[文法点] －3点
[総評] time「時間」は不可算名詞だが、形容詞がついて限定されると可算名詞扱い。
こうした基本はしっかり学びたい。

[モニター答案例2] [15 / 25点]

Machine translation today is accurate and will be ✕ used in important business
　　　　　　　✕ →has become：減点なし　　　ヌケ→more widely：－1点

negotiations. With machine translation, you need less time and less money for
　　　　　　✕ →It saves：－3点　　　　　　　　　　　　✕ →money：－1点

translation, which is the biggest advantage. However, machines cannot read
　　　✕ →トル：－1点　　　　　　　✕ →understand cultural backgrounds：内容点で減点

information out of the text, so the translation is sometimes wrong.　(45 words)

[内容点] 第1段落は英語として不十分な部分があるが、内容としては❶❷ともにOK
とする。第2段落は、❶❷ともにOKだが、英語として不十分・不自然な部分は文法点
での減点とする。第3段落は❶が不可で－4点。❷はOK。以上、－4点。

［文法点］－6点。
［総評］全体としてまずまずだが、最終文前半のような捏造は厳に慎むこと。

STEP3
ネイティブスピーカーの答案に学ぶ

模範解答

Recent years have seen notable improvements in the accuracy of machine translation, leading to increased adoption by companies. Although this technology is not new, until recently inaccuracies limited its use. Its primary benefit lies in the almost instantaneous translation of documents, which saves time and costs. However, human translators remain superior in conveying cultural nuances.　(55 words)

近年、機械翻訳の精度に著しい向上が見られ、企業による導入が進んでいる。この技術は新しいものではないが、最近まで精度の低さから、その利用は限られていた。機械翻訳の主な利点は、ほぼ瞬時に文書を翻訳できるため、時間とコストを節約できることだ。しかし、文化的なニュアンスを伝えるという点では、依然として人間の翻訳者の方が優れている。

語彙リスト

□ 1.	nótable	形	注目に値する、著しい
□ 2.	adóption	名	採用
□ 3.	prímary	形	主な
□ 4.	lie in ～	熟	～にある
□ 5.	instantáneous	形	瞬時の
□ 6.	remáin ～	動	～のままである
□ 7.	convéy ～	動	～を伝える

解答例

The popularity of electric kick scooters is growing because they are environmentally friendly and relatively quiet. They are also easy to store and carry around. However, they can be dangerous when used at high speed and are not suitable for use on rainy days, carrying large items or traveling long distances.

(51 words)

電動キックスクーターは環境に優しく、音も比較的静かなため、人気が高まっている。収納や持ち運びも簡単だ。しかし、高速で使用すると危険なこともあり、雨の日の使用や大きな荷物の運搬、長距離の移動には適していない。

STEP 1
問 題 文 の 要 点 を つ か む

第1段落

Electric kick scooters, or electric kickboards, are gradually changing the way people get around every day around the world. Some people buy gasoline-powered cars and motorcycles, but these scooters are becoming more popular due to their convenience and other reasons.

電動キックスクーター、つまり電動キックボードは、世界中の人々の日々の移動手段を徐々に変えつつある。ガソリン車やバイクを購入する人もいるが、こうしたスクーターはその利便性や他の理由で人気が高まっている。

語彙リスト

□ **1.**	electric kick scooter	名	電動キックスクーター
			※kick を省くことも多い。electric kickboard「電動キックボード」とほぼ同じ意味で使われる。
□ **2.**	grádually	副	徐々に
□ **3.**	the way SV	熟	SVのやり方
□ **4.**	get around	熟	(街などで) あちこち移動する
□ **5.**	gásoline-pówered car	名	ガソリン車
□ **6.**	due to ～	熟	～が原因で　※このtoは前置詞。

解説と要旨

この段落では「電動キックスクーターの人気が高まっている」ということが述べられています。それ以外の情報は無視してもよいでしょう。8点満点で、減点法で採点します。

[**要約例**] The popularity of electric kick scooters is growing.
「電動キックスクーターの人気が高まっている」

第2段落

What kind of benefits do the electric kickboards have? Since they are powered by electricity, they are less harmful to the environment than gas-powered vehicles. In addition, their motors produce very little noise compared to engines. Furthermore, they are more compact than ordinary bicycles, so they can be easily stored and carried around.

　そうした電動キックボードにはどんなメリットがあるのだろうか。電気を動力源としているため、ガソリン車に比べて環境への害が少ない。また、モーターが出す音もエンジンに比べて非常に小さい。さらに、それらは普通の自転車よりもコンパクトなので、収納や持ち運びも簡単だ。

語彙リスト

□ **7.**	be hármful to ～	熟	～に有害である
□ **8.**	véhicle	名	車両
□ **9.**	compáred to ～	熟	～と比べて　※受動態の分詞構文
□ **10.**	cárry ～ aróund	熟	～を（あちこち）持ち運ぶ

解説と要旨

　ここでは電動スクーター(本文では「電動キックボード」と言い換えている) のプラス面が3つ述べられています。それは、❶「環境への害が少ない」、❷「静かだ」、❸「収納や持ち運びが簡単だ」です。9点満点で、各区分3点として減点法で採点します。
[要約例] ... because they are environmentally friendly and relatively quiet. They are also easy to store and carry around.
「電動スクーターは環境に優しく、音も比較的静かなため (、人気が高まっている)。収納や持ち運びも簡単だ」
[注1] environmentally friendly「環境に優しい」は eco-friendly や better for the environment などでも可。
[注2]「～は騒音が少ない」は make less noise や be less noisy とすることもできる。
[注3] carry の代わりに transport「(車両に乗せて) ～を運ぶ」は不可。

One weak point is they are capable of reaching speeds of more than 30 mph and can be very dangerous. In fact, accidents involving them have resulted in death. Also, since they have no roof, they cannot be used on rainy days. Since they have no basket, they cannot carry large items. Finally, they are not vehicles suitable for long-distance travel because they are smaller than gasoline-powered motorbikes.

弱点の1つは、時速30マイル以上のスピードが出せるため、非常に危険になりうることが挙げられる。実際、これらが絡む死亡事故も起きている。また、屋根がないので雨の日には使えない。カゴがないため、大きな荷物は運べない。最後に、ガソリンで動くバイクより小さいため、長距離移動に適した車両ではない。

語彙リスト

□	11.	be cápable of ～	熟 ～の能力がある
	12.	～ mph	名 時速～マイル（= mile per hour）
	13.	invólve ～	動 ～を巻き込む、～を伴う
	14.	resúlt in ～	熟 ～という結果をもたらす
	15.	long-dístance	形 長距離の

解説と要旨

　この段落では電動スクーターのマイナス面が4つ述べられています。それらは、❶「高速で使用すると危険になりうる」、❷「雨の日の使用には適していない」、❸「大きな荷物の運搬には適していない」、❹「長距離の移動には適していない」です。8点満点で各区分2点として減点法で採点します。

[要約例] However, they can be dangerous when used at high speed and are not suitable for use on rainy days, carrying large items or traveling long distances.

「しかし、高速で使用すると危険なこともあり、雨の日の使用や大きな荷物の運搬、長距離の移動には適していない」

[注1] when used は when they are used から they are が省略された形。

[注2] items は loads「荷物」でも可。

STEP 2
モニター答案でポイントをつかむ

[**モニター答案例1**] [**23 / 25点**]

Electric scooters are becoming more common because they are ecofriendly

and produce less noise than engines and it is easy to store and carry them. However,

          △ →they are easy to store and carry：減点なし

they are sometimes dangerous ✕ and are not suitable for riding on rainy days,

     ヌケ→when used at high speed：−1点

carrying large baggages and going to faraway places.   (47 words)

   ✕ →things：−1点

[**内容点**] 第1段落はOK。第2段落は❶❷❸すべてOK。第3段落は、❶は不十分だが文法点での減点とする。❷はOK。❸は不十分だが文法点での減点とする。❹はOK。以上、内容点での減点はない。

[**文法点**] −2点。it is easy to store and carry them では、旧情報のthem が文末にあり不自然。they are easy to store and carry とすると旧情報のthey が文頭に移動し流れがよくなる（この構文に使われる代表的形容詞はeasy / difficult / tough なので、「タフ構文」と呼ばれている）。

[**総評**] baggage「手荷物、旅行荷物」は本来多くのカバンの集合体だったので、不可算名詞の扱い。1つのカバンと言いたい時はa piece of baggage とする。

[**モニター答案例2**] [**17 / 25点**]

More and more people are using electric scooters because they are

ecofriendly, less noisy, and smaller than gas-powered vehicles. However, they run

more slowly, can be very dangerous, are useless on rainy days, cannot carry heavy

✕ →when used at high speed：−1点　　　　　✕ →offer no protection from rain：内容点で減点

baggages, and are not preferred than going to a distant place.   (47 words)

✕ →things：−1点　　　✕ →good for：−2点　　　△ →distant places：減点なし

078

［**内容点**］第１段落はOK。第２段落は❶❷はOKだが、❸は具体化が必要で、－２点。第３段落は、❶は不十分だが文法点での減点とする。❷は不十分で－２点。❸❹は文法点での減点はあるがOK。以上、－４点。

［**文法点**］－４点。a distant place は「ある１つの遠い場所」の意味になる。ここでは一般論なので複数形が適切。prefer は、prefer A to B ～で「BよりAの方を好む」の意味。

［**総評**］useless では「どの点で役立たずなのか」という疑問が残る。英語では「とことん説明する」という姿勢が重要。

STEP**3**
ネイティブスピーカーの答案に学ぶ

模範解答

Electric-powered kick scooters are gaining worldwide popularity for several reasons, including convenience, sustainability, quiet running noise, and portability. However, since kick scooters can travel quite fast, they can be the cause of fatal accidents. Being roofless and storage-less also restricts their use, and their small size limits the distances they can travel.

(52 words)

電動キックスクーターは、利便性、持続可能性、静かな走行音、携帯性など、いくつかの理由から世界的な人気を集めている。しかし、キックスクーターはかなりのスピードで走行できるため、死亡事故の原因となることもある。また、屋根がなく、収納もついていないため、用途には制限があり、サイズも小さいため、移動できる距離も限られている。

語彙リスト

□			
□ **1.**	sustainabílity	图	持続可能性
□ **2.**	portabílity	图	携帯性
□ **3.**	fátal áccident	图	死亡事故
□ **4.**	restríct ～	動	～を制限する

解 答 例

In Tallinn, public transportation became basically free of charge for its residents in 2013. This was expected to bring financial and environmental benefits and improve the mobility of people with low incomes. However, while there was some success in the latter, there was not much effect on the former. In France, many people are against free fares, believing the loss of revenue would result in a heavier burden on taxpayers.

(70 words)

2013年、タリンの住民は公共交通機関を基本的に無料で利用できるようになった。これは、財政的、環境的な利益をもたらし、低所得者の移動を改善するものと思われていた。しかし、後者の改善では一定の成果があったが、前者に関してはさほど効果が見られなかった。フランスでは、収入減は納税者の負担を重くすると考え、運賃無料化に反対する人が多い。

STEP 1
問題文の要点をつかむ

第 1 段 落

In 2013, public transportation became free in Tallinn, the capital of Estonia. Before that, free public transportation initiatives had been implemented only in relatively small municipalities and never in a capital city. Under the initiative, only registered residents can purchase a "green card" for two euros, and with that, all buses, streetcars, and trolleybuses in the city are free of charge.

2013年、エストニアの首都タリンで公共交通機関が無料化された。それまでは、公共交通機関の無料化という取り組みは比較的小さな自治体でのみ実施されており、首都で実施されたことはなかった。この取り組みでは、住民登録をしている人だけが2ユーロで「グリーンカード」を購入でき、これを持っていれば市内のバス、路面電車、トロリーバスがすべて無料になる。

語彙リスト

☐ **1.**	inítiative	名	新構想、取り組み
☐ **2.**	ímplemènt ～	動	～を実施する
☐ **3.**	rélatively	副	比較的
☐ **4.**	mùnicipálity	名	地方自治体
☐ **5.**	régistered résident	名	住民登録をしている住民
☐ **6.**	púrchase A for B	熟	B（金額）を出してAを購入する
☐ **7.**	free of charge	熟	無料で

解説と要旨

　第1～3文から、❶「2013年に」、❷「(エストニアの首都の) タリンの市民を対象として」、❸「公共交通が無料化された」という内容を書けばよいでしょう。時と場所は必ず明示すること。第3文にある「住民登録している」は、❷「タリンの市民」で十分です。また、語数制限を考えると「グリーンカード」などの具体的な内容を書くこと

は無理でしょう。9点満点で、各区分3点として減点法で採点します。

[**要約例**] In Tallinn, public transportation became basically free of charge for its residents in 2013.

「2013年、タリンの住民は公共交通機関を基本的に無料で利用できるようになった」

[**注1**] transportation は不可算名詞である。

[**注2**] in 2013 があるので過去時制を用いること。

第2段落

These initiatives were expected to bring benefits, such as increased tax revenues due to a population increase for free rides, reduced equipment costs for railway companies, contributing to a better environment due to reduced number of cars, and improved mobility for low-income people.

こうした取り組みにより、無料乗車がもたらす人口増加による税収増、鉄道会社にとっての設備コスト削減、自動車台数の減少による環境改善への貢献、低所得者の移動の利便性向上などのメリットが期待されていた。

語彙リスト

☐ **8.**	tax révenue	名	税収
☐ **9.**	equípment cost	名	設備コスト
☐ **10.**	mobílity	名	移動しやすさ

解説と要旨

骨格となるのは❶「財政面での恩恵」、❷「環境改善」、❸「低所得者の移動の便の向上」、❹「❶❷❸が期待されていた」です。「無料乗車がもたらす人口増加による税収増、鉄道会社にとっての設備コスト削減」は❶でまとめます。「自動車台数の減少による環境改善」は「環境改善」などと抽象化して❷でまとめ、語数を抑えるとよいでしょう。8点満点で、各区分2点として減点法で採点します。

[**要約例**] This was expected to bring financial and environmental benefits and improve the mobility of people with low incomes.

「これは、財政的、環境的な利益をもたらし、低所得者の移動の便を改善するものと思われていた」

[**注1**] bring financial and environmental benefits は、solve [deal with] financial and environmental problems とすることもできる。

[注2] people with low incomes は poor people では言い換えられない。poor は、その日の食べ物にも困るぐらい貧困であることを示唆する語である。

第 3 段 落

According to a 2014 survey, it is true that the number of times Tallinn residents walked on foot decreased by 40%. However, the number of times they traveled by car decreased by only 5%. Apparently, the effect on gas emissions was not as large as had been expected. And of course, this does not seem to be suitable for every city. For example, in Paris, France, there are many people who oppose the idea of free fares, believing that it would simply lead to a reduction in fare revenues, which would ultimately increase the burden on taxpayers.

2014年の調査によると、確かにタリン市民の徒歩での移動回数は40%減少した。しかし、自動車での移動回数は5%しか減少していない。どうやらガス排出量への影響は予想されたほど大きくなかったようである。そしてもちろん、これはすべての都市に適しているわけではないようである。例えばフランスのパリでは、運賃無料化という考えは単に運賃収入の減少につながり、結果的に納税者の負担を増やすだけだと信じて反対する人が多い。

語彙リスト

☐ 11.	súrvey	名	（アンケート）調査
☐ 12.	appárently	副	どうやら…らしい
☐ 13.	redúction	名	減少
☐ 14.	fare révenue	名	運賃収入
☐ 15.	últimately	副	最終的には
☐ 16.	búrden	名	負担
☐ 17.	táxpàyer	名	納税者

骨格となるのは❶「（タリン市民の）移動性の改善には一定の成果があった」、❷「（自動車の使用はわずか5%しか減少しなかったため）ガスの排出量はさほど減少しなかった（＝環境面での効果は少なかった）」、❸「フランスでは運賃無料化に反対する人が多い」、❹「納税者の負担が増えるから」です。語数を抑えるため、前文に言及する形でimprove the mobility of people with low incomesをthe latter（後者）で、bring financial and environmental benefitsをthe former（前者）で表すとよいでしょう。エストニアとフランスの例をまとめ、最初に「運賃無料化への各国政府の取り組みは、困難に直面している」The efforts of national governments to provide free fares have been fraught with difficulties.とすれば全体がうまくまとまります。ただし、今回に関しては語数の関係で省いた方がいいでしょう。8点満点で、各区分2点として減点法で採点します。

[**要約例**] However, while there was some success in the latter, there was not much effect on the former. In France, many people are against free fares, believing the loss of revenue would result in a heavier burden on taxpayers.

「しかし、後者の改善では一定の成果があったが、前者に関してはさほど効果が見られなかった。フランスでは、収入減は納税者の負担を重くすると考え、運賃無料化に反対する人が多い」

STEP 2
モニター答案でポイントをつかむ

[モニター答案例1]［17 / 25点］

In Tallinn, registered residents have been able to use most of the public

transportation for almost free since 2013. People expected that this idea would

help <u>improve</u> financial and environmental problems. However, it did not work

✗ →solve（problems とのコロケーション）：−2点

well. A survey in 2014 showed that the gas emissions did not decrease so much.

People in Paris are also objecting ✕ the idea because it can make <u>financial</u> problems

ヌケ→to：−1点   ✕ →tax：内容点で減点

worse. (66 words)

［**内容点**］第1段落❶❷❸はOK。第2段落は❶❷❹OK。❸がヌケで−2点。第3段落
❶がヌケで−2点、❷❸はOKだが、❹は納税負担に言及できていないので−1点。以
上、−5点。
［**文法点**］−3点。object to 〜は「〜に反対する」の意味というより「〜を嫌がる」と
いう主観的な言い方なので、oppose / be opposed toを用いたい。
［**総評**］本番でこれぐらい出来ていれば合格点はもらえるだろう。

［**モニター答案例2**］［**3 / 25点**］

In Tallinn, the capital of Estonia, public transportation <u>become</u> free. By

✕ →became：−2点

registering for 2 euros, they can use all buses ✕ streetcars for nothing. This idea

ヌケ→and：−1点

was expected to be beneficial for <u>a</u> society such as <u>increase</u> tax revenues. However,

✕ →トル：−1点   ✕ →increased：−2点

unfortunately, the number of times they traveled by car decreased by only 5%. In

Paris in France, many people oppose the idea because <u>this</u> could increase the burden

✕ →it：−1点

on taxpayers due to a reduction in fare revenues. (76 words)

［**内容点**］語数制限を6語オーバーしているので−6点。第1段落❶のヌケで−3点。❷
❸はOK。第2段落❶❹はOK。❷❸ヌケで−4点。第3段落❶のヌケで−2点。❷❸
❹はOK。以上、−15点。
［**文法点**］−7点。
［**総評**］そもそも語数オーバーで6点も減点されたのが残念。

準
1
級

01

085

模範解答

　In 2013, Tallinn made public transportation free for registered residents. Expected benefits included increased tax revenue and a positive environmental impact. However, a resident survey revealed only minimal reduction in car use, indicating some anticipated environmental benefits did not fully materialize. This raised concerns in other cities such as Paris, where free fares are opposed on the grounds of revenue loss and increased taxpayer burden.

(65 words)

　2013年、タリンでは住民登録をしている人に対し公共交通機関を無料化した。見込まれていた効果は、税収の増加や環境への好影響であった。しかし、住民調査の結果、自動車利用はわずかな減少にとどまったことが明らかになり、環境面で期待された恩恵が十分に得られなかったことが示された。このことにより、減収や納税者の負担増を理由に運賃無料化に反対しているパリのような他の都市でも懸念が生じることとなった。

語彙リスト

□ **1.**	matérialize	動	実現する
□ **2.**	raise concérns	熟	懸念を生じさせる
□ **3.**	táxpayer bùrden	名	納税者の負担
□ **4.**	on the grounds of ～	熟	～という理由で

解答例

　　The coronavirus pandemic stirred up debate about conditions in the workplace. Belgium introduced a four-day workweek in 2022 which the government stated would create a better work-life balance for citizens, and stimulate the economy. However, some people oppose the idea because the total number of working hours may not be reduced, making each working day much longer, and shift workers complain they will not benefit from the new system.

(69 words)

　　コロナウイルスの大流行は、職場の状況について議論を巻き起こした。ベルギー政府は2022年に週休3日制を導入したが、政府の見解ではこれは、市民のための仕事と家庭生活のバランスを改善し、経済を活性化させるということだ。しかし、総労働時間が短縮されない可能性があるため、1日あたりの労働時間が大幅に長くなるかもしれないと、この考えに反対する声もある。また、シフト勤務者はこの新制度から恩恵を受けられないと不平を述べている。

STEP 1
問題文の要点をつかむ

第1段落

　　Portugal followed the example of Belgium and the United Kingdom by announcing the introduction of a four-day workweek on a trial basis. Debate over the four-day workweek has been heating up thanks to the virus outbreak, which prompted workers and employers to rethink the importance of workplace flexibility and benefits.

準1級

02

　　ポルトガルはベルギーとイギリスの例にならい、試験的に週休3日制の導入を発表した。週休3日制をめぐる議論は、労働者と雇用主が職場の柔軟性と福利厚生の重要性を再考するきっかけとなったウイルスの流行によって、ますます熱を帯びてきている。

語彙リスト

□ **1.**	fóllow the exámples of 〜	熟	〜の例にならう
□ **2.**	the Uníted Kíngdom	名	イギリス、英国
□ **3.**	a four-day wórkwèek	熟	週4日労働制、週休3日制
□ **4.**	on a trial básis	熟	試験的に
			※on a 〜 basis で副詞句を作る。
□ **5.**	prompt (O) to (V)	動	(O) に (V) するよう促す
□ **6.**	flèxibílity	名	柔軟性
□ **7.**	bénefits	名	福利厚生　※この意味では複数形。

解説と要旨

　　第2段落、第3段落はベルギーの話がされているので、ポルトガル、イギリスの話は特に必要なく、また語数制限があるため、これを要約に入れる余裕はありません。週休3日制については、第2段落の要約に含めるとよいでしょう。この段落では❶「（コロナ）ウイルスの流行により」、❷「職場の状況についての」、❸「議論が巻き起こっ

た」を要約に含めれば十分です。「ウイルスの流行の結果、週休3日制が導入された」とするのは、やや乱暴です。8点満点で、各区分3点として減点法で採点します。0点になった場合、それ以上減点はしません。

[要約例] The coronavirus pandemic stirred up debate about conditions in the workplace.

「コロナウイルスの大流行は、職場の状況について議論を巻き起こした」

[注1]「大流行」は pandemic とする。the coronavirus pandemic は the COVID-19 pandemic も可。あるいは本文のまま the virus outbreak としてもよい。

[注2] stir up「(騒ぎ) を起こす」は、generate、arouse、spark などでも可。

[注3] debate は、ここでは「漠然とした議論」の意味で不可算名詞の扱い。a debate でも×ではない。

[注4]「職場の状況」は、working conditions、conditions in the workplace など。

[注5] 主語を「人々」として because of the coronavirus pandemic, many people began [started] to discuss [rethink] ～としてもよい。

第2段落

Belgium became the first European country to legalize a four-day workweek. In February 2022, Belgian employees who would normally work five days a week won the right to a four-day workweek without a cut in pay. Belgian Prime Minister Alexander De Croo said the changes should help Belgians find it easier to combine their family lives and careers, creating a more dynamic economy.

ベルギーはヨーロッパ諸国の中で初めて週休3日制を合法化した国となった。2022年2月、通常週5日働いていたベルギーの労働者は、減給なしで週休3日制の権利を獲得した。ベルギーのアレクサンダー・ドゥ・クロー首相は、この変更によってベルギー国民が家庭生活と仕事を両立しやすくなり、より活発な経済が生まれるはずだと述べた。

語彙リスト

☐ 8.	légalize ～	動	～を合法化する
☐ 9.	combíne A and B	熟	AとBを組み合わせる
☐ 10.	dynámic	形	動的な、活発な

　第1～2文をまとめれば❶「2022年ベルギーは週休3日制を導入した」となります。これに対する政府の見解である第3文は、❷「政府はそれにより家庭生活と仕事のバランスをとり」、❸「経済を活性化させるとしている」とまとめます。9点満点で各区分3点として減点法で採点します。

[**要　約　例**] Belgium introduced a four-day workweek in 2022 which the government stated would create a better work-life balance for citizens, and stimulate the economy.

　「ベルギー政府は2022年に週休3日制を導入したが、政府の見解ではこれは、市民のための仕事と家庭生活のバランスを改善し、経済を活性化させるということだ」

[**注1**] introduce ～を、別の表現で書けば bring ～ into use for the first time となるが、語数が増えすぎるので introduce のままでよいだろう。

[**注2**]「家庭生活と仕事のバランスをとる」は、create [find / strike] a better work-life balance が定型。improve a work-life balance でも可。

[**注3**] stimulate は「～を刺激する」という意味。「より活発な経済を生む」は、stimulate [boost / revitalize / dynamize] the economy とする。

第3段落

　However, the idea of a four-day workweek is not popular with everyone. For instance, some full-time employees, who already work full days, are opposed to the idea of working even longer hours on the days they work, saying that working days may be reduced, but they will be condensed into fewer days. What's more, those who take shifts complain that they will not be able to take advantage of the flexibility.

　しかし、週休3日制の考えは万人に受け入れられていない。例えば、すでに1日を目いっぱい働いているフルタイムの労働者の中には、就業日にさらに長時間働くことに反対する人もいる。労働日数は減るかもしれないが、より少ない日数に詰め込まれると言うのだ。さらに、シフト制で働いている労働者からは、その柔軟性を活かすことができないと不満の声が上がっている。

語彙リスト

☐ **11.**	be oppósed to ～	熟	～に反対している
☐ **12.**	be condénsed into ～	熟	～に凝縮される

☐ **13.**	take shifts	熟	シフト制で働く
☐ **14.**	take advántage of 〜	熟	〜を利用する

　第１文は**❶**「この考え（週休３日制）に反対する人がいる」とし、その理由の例である第２文は、**❷**「労働日数は減っても、１日の労働時間が大幅に長くなる」とします。さらに第３文にある**❸**「シフト勤務者は新制度の恩恵を受けられないと不平を述べている」を追加すればよいでしょう。本文にある「新制度の柔軟性を利用できない」は「新制度から恩恵を得られない」とすれば内容として十分です。８点満点で、各区分３点として減点法で採点します。０点になった場合、それ以上減点はしません。

［要約例］However, some people oppose the idea because the total number of working hours may not be reduced, making each working day much longer, and shift workers complain they will not benefit from the new system.

　「しかし、総労働時間が短縮されない可能性があるため、１日あたりの労働時間が大幅に長くなるかもしれないと、この考えに反対する声もある。また、シフト勤務者はこの新制度から恩恵を受けられないと不平を述べている」

［注１］「〜に反対する」は、oppose / be opposed to / be against 〜など。

［注２］「１日の労働時間が長くなる」という英語は、they will work more hours on each day などでもよい。

STEP **2**
モ ニ タ ー 答 案 で ポ イ ン ト を つ か む

[モニター答案例1] [10 / 25点]

　　Because of the pandemic, many people began to consider a four-day workweek. It may make work flexible. In Belgium, workers can earn as much money as before in four-day workweek. It is said that they can find a good balance

✗ →for：−2点

between work and pleasure, and it is good for the economy. However, there are

✗ →family life：内容点で減点

some people who oppose the idea because they <u>cannot work</u> longer in a day.

✗ → do not want to work：内容点で減点

(68 words)

［**内容点**］第1段落の**❶❸**はOK。**❷**は「コロナウイルスの大流行」→「職場の状況の再考」→「週休3日制」という流れを無視しているので−3点。第2段落は**❶**が不十分なため−2点、**❷**はpleasureではなくfamily lifeの間違いで−3点、**❸**はOK。「ベルギーの労働者は、減給なしで週4日制の権利を獲得した」の部分を書いているが、不要である。第3段落の**❶**はOK。**❷**は不十分。cannot workではなくdo not want to workなので−2点。**❸**のヌケで−3点。以上、−13点。

［**文法点**］−2点。

［**総評**］文法的なミスは少ないが、英文内容の把握が不十分。まずは各段落の内容把握を正確に。

［**モニター答案例2**］［**14 / 25点**］

　　Portugal introduced a four-day workweek, which had been already adopted by Belgium and the U.K., as a trial. One reason for that is that people rethought the importance of workplace flexibility and benefits through the virus outbreak. In 2022, Belgium began to legalize it without reducing <u>worker's</u> salary. The Prime

✗ → workers'：−2点

Minister believed it would create a more dynamic economy. However, many people oppose this idea.

(65 words)

［**内容点**］第1段落の**❶❷❸**はすべてOK。答案例の第1文は不要であり、ここで語数を使ってしまったため、後半が不十分な記述になってしまっている。第2段落は**❶**はOK。**❷**がヌケで−3点。**❸**はOK。第3段落は**❶**はOKだが、**❷❸**のヌケで−6点。以上、−9点。

［**文法点**］−2点。

［**総評**］各段落の語数のバランスを考えないと、このように後半が不十分になる。必ず全体のバランスを考えてから書き始めること。

模範解答

   Portugal became the third European nation to trial a four-day workweek, a concept that gained more recognition during the pandemic, when the work-life balance was reexamined. In 2022, Belgium legalized the right to work four days rather than five for equal salary, though this could mean each workday had more hours. This is one reason, along with the complaints of shift workers, that the system is not without its critics.

(70 words)

   ポルトガルは、週休3日制を試行した欧州で3番目の国になった。この制度はワークライフバランスが見直されたコロナの大流行の時により認識されるようになった。2022年には、ベルギーが同一賃金で5日間ではなく4日間働く権利を合法化した。だが、これは1日の労働時間が延長されうることを意味した。これは、シフト勤務者の不満とともに、この制度に批判がないわけではない理由の一つである。

語彙リスト

- ☐ **1.** reexámine 〜　　　動 〜を見直す
- ☐ **2.** along with 〜　　　熟 〜とともに

解 答 例

Recently, unstaffed convenience stores have become common in parts of Asia. The use of machines saves customers considerable time and the store saves money on labor costs. Furthermore, the latest technology helps the store to manage products and monitor sales figures. However, introducing the equipment and technology is extremely costly and there are potential problems with food hygiene and the safety and cleanliness of the store.

(66 words)

　最近、アジアの一部では無人のコンビニエンスストアが一般的になっている。機械を使用することで、客はかなりの時間を節約でき、店は人件費を節約できる。さらに、最新のテクノロジーは店の商品管理や売上高のチェックに役立っている。しかし、そうした設備や技術の導入には莫大な費用がかかり、食品衛生や店舗の安全性、清潔さにも問題がある可能性がある。

STEP 1
問題文の要点をつかむ

第1段落

In recent years, unstaffed convenience stores have become common in Asian countries, such as China, Japan, and Singapore. In an unstaffed convenience store, machines perform basic operations in the store, and there are no store clerks.

近年、中国、日本、シンガポールなどのアジア諸国では、無人のコンビニエンスストアが一般的になっている。無人コンビニでは、店内の基本的な業務は機械が行い、店員はいない。

語彙リスト

□ **1.** unstáffed　　　　　　形 店員がいない

解説と要旨

　第1段落は第1文だけで主張を網羅することができます。「中国、日本、シンガポールなどのアジア諸国」は「アジアの一部で」とまとめればよいでしょう。in Asia「アジアで」では不十分です。❶「最近、アジアの一部で」、❷「無人のコンビニエンスストアが一般的になっている」とします。第2文は「無人」であることの説明にすぎないので要約には不要です。8点満点で、各区分4点として減点法で採点します。

[**要 約 例**] Recently, unstaffed convenience stores have become common in parts of Asia.

　「最近、アジアの一部では無人のコンビニエンスストアが一般的になっている」

[**注1**]「〜が一般的になっている」は、the number of 〜 has increased、there are many 〜など数に変換してもよい。またit is not unusual to find 〜とすることもできる。

[**注2**] unstaffedを言い換えるならunattendedとなる。unmannedは、性別に関するPCの観点から避けるべき語。

[**注3**]「アジア諸国で」は、in some Asian countriesでもよい。

At unstaffed convenience stores, customers simply swipe their mobile phones to enter, select and pick up items, pay using self-service registers, and leave. That way, people can save a lot of time. The benefits to the shop are that labor costs are greatly reduced. Cutting-edge technology makes it easier to manage products, and it is possible to monitor the purchase, inventory, and sales status of products.

無人のコンビニエンスストアでは、客は携帯電話をスワイプするだけで入店し、商品を選んで手に取り、セルフレジで支払いを済ませて店を出る。こうすることで、人々は時間を大幅に節約できる。店にとっての利点は、人件費が大幅に削減されることだ。最先端技術により商品管理も容易になり、商品の仕入れ、在庫、商品の販売状況をチェックすることができる。

語彙リスト

☐ 2.	swipe ~	動	~をスワイプする、読み取り機に通す
☐ 3.	sélf-sérvice régister	名	セルフレジ
☐ 4.	lábor cost	名	人件費
☐ 5.	cútting-édge	形	最先端の
☐ 6.	mónitor ~	動	~を監視する、チェックする
☐ 7.	púrchase	名	仕入れ ※この意味では不可算名詞。
☐ 8.	invéntory	名	在庫（品）
☐ 9.	sáles státus	名	販売状況 ※status quo「現状」

解説と要旨

　第1文は、無人のコンビニエンスストアで客がすることが書かれています。語数を考えれば❶「顧客は機械を使って」ぐらいで十分です。第2文は❷「(顧客は)多くの時間を節約できる」とします。第3文については❸「店は人件費を節約できる」とすれば十分です。第4文は❹「最新の技術は商品管理や売上高のチェックに役立っている」とすればよいでしょう。8点満点で、各区分2点として減点法で採点します。

［要 約 例］The use of machines saves customers considerable time and the store saves money on labor costs. Furthermore, the latest technology helps the store to manage products and monitor sales figures.

　「機械を使用することで、客はかなりの時間を節約でき、店は人件費を節約できる。さらに、最新のテクノロジーは店の商品管理や売上高のチェックに役立っている」

[注1] save は、他動詞で「〜を節約する」という意味のほか、〈save＋人＋もの〉の形をとり、「〈人〉の〈金や時間〉を節約する」という意味になる。

[注2]「人件費」は labor costs 又は personnel expenses。

[注3]「商品を管理する」は、manage [keep track of] products。

[注4]「売上高のチェック」は、本文通り monitor 〜「（一定期間にわたり）〜を監視する」を使うのが最適である。

第 3 段 落

Despite these advantages, there are a lot of problems to overcome as well. A large amount of money is required for the introduction of equipment and technology. Not only are there food hygiene and safety issues, but also there is the issue of cleanliness. There may be dust on the product shelves, or when people enter the store from outside on a rainy day, the floor may get dirty. These are the issues that unstaffed convenience stores have to deal with.

こうした利点があるにもかかわらず、克服すべき問題も多い。設備や技術の導入には多額の資金が必要となる。食品の衛生や安全性の問題だけでなく、清潔さの問題もある。商品棚にホコリが溜まったり、雨の日に外から人が入ると床が汚れたりするかもしれない。これらは無人のコンビニエンスストアが対処しなければならない問題である。

語彙リスト

☐ **10.**	as well	熟	また
☐ **11.**	equípment	名	設備　＊不可算名詞。
☐ **12.**	not only 〜 , but also ...	熟	〜だけでなく…もまた
			※ not only が文頭にくる場合は倒置の形にするという決まりがある。
☐ **13.**	hýgiene	名	衛生
☐ **14.**	cléanliness	名	清潔さ

解説と要旨

第1文は、抽象論なので要約では省いても問題ありません。第2文は、主語を入れ替えて❶「そうした設備や技術の導入には莫大な費用がかかる」とします。第3文は❷「食品衛生や店舗の安全性、清潔さにも問題がある」とします。第4〜5文は第1〜

3文の具体化なので省略します。9点満点で、❶は4点、❷は5点として、減点法で採点します。

[要約例] However, introducing the equipment and technology is extremely costly and there are potential problems with food hygiene and the safety and cleanliness of the store.

「しかし、そうした設備や技術の導入には莫大な費用がかかり、食品衛生や店舗の安全性、清潔さにも問題がある可能性がある」

[注1]「～には莫大な費用がかかる」は、～ is very costlyや～ costs a lot of money など。

[注2]「食品衛生」は、food hygiene [sanitation] とする。

[注3]「～の問題」は、～ problem [issue]、problem with ～など。

STEP 2
モニター答案でポイントをつかむ

[モニター答案例1] [8 / 25点]

　　Today, there are many unstaffed convenience stores, in which store clerks are replaced with machines. These stores benefit customers because they have only to use their mobile phones and pay using self-service registers to buy what they want. Also, they benefit the shops by cutting labor costs. On the contrary, many

✗ →By contrast：-3点

✗ problems, such as cleanliness, food hygiene and safety issues, remain to be

ヌケ→potential：-2点

solved.
(64 words)

[内容点] 第1段落の❶は「アジアの一部で」のヌケで-4点。❷はOK。in which 以下の記述は不要である。第2段落の❶はOK。❷がヌケで-2点。❸はOK。❹のヌケで-2点。第3段落の❶がヌケで-4点。❷はOK。以上、-12点。

［**文法点**］－5点。on the contrary は、否定文に続けて「それどころか」の意味で使うのが一般的である。ここでは by [in] contrast「一方」とすべきであろう。また、potential がないと「必ず問題が起きる」という意味になる。

［**総評**］内容吟味が不十分である。「言いたいことをざっくり書く」のでは合格点には至らない。各文の内容を精査して要・不要を判断する必要がある。

［モニター答案例2］［0 / 25点］

More and more convenience stores whose employees are not humans, but

✕ →unstaffed convenience stores：－3点

machines, have ✕introduced in Asian countries. The stores can save not only time

ヌケ→been：－3点 ✕ →can not only save customers time and trouble：－3点

and trouble of customers but also their own labor costs. However, there are some

ヌケ→potential：－2点 ✕ →lower：－3点

✕problems. It cost ✕large amount of money to start✕. Moreover, managers

✕ →costs：－1点 ヌケ→a：－1点 ヌケ→a store：－2点

should think about how to keep food, hygiene and the way of keeping the store clean.

✕ →there are problems with hygiene, safety, and cleanliness：－3点

(65 words)

［**内容点**］第1段落の❶は「近年」「アジアの一部で」のヌケで－2点。❷は不可。machines は employees ではないので、全面的な書き直しが必要である。－4点。第2段落の❶❷は save の用法が間違っているので、文法点で減点することにする。❸も save their own labor costs では不可。lower labor costs「人件費を下げる」とする。これも文法点での減点とする。❹のヌケで－2点。第3段落の❶は OK だが文法点での減点がある。❷は原文と離れているので不可だが、これも文法点としての減点とする。以上、－8点。

［**文法点**］－21点。employee は「人間の従業員」の意味なので第1文は不自然。

［**総評**］これほど多くの文法的なミスをしていたのでは、作文にはならない。

STEP 3
ネイティブスピーカーの解答に学ぶ

模範解答

Recently parts of Asia have seen an increase in unstaffed convenience stores, where customers can complete various transactions at automated terminals. This often saves customers' time, as well as reducing labor costs and streamlining stock management for the stores. However, automated systems are considerably expensive to install, and unstaffed stores pose problems in maintaining a clean and sanitary shopping environment, so this new retail style still has issues to address.

(70 words)

最近、アジアの一部では、客が自動化された端末で、さまざまな取引を完了することができる無人のコンビニエンスストアが増えている。これは客の時間の節約になることが多いだけでなく、店にとっても人件費削減や在庫管理の合理化にもつながる。しかし、自動化システムの導入にはかなりのコストがかかるし、無人店舗は清潔で衛生的な買い物環境を維持するのに問題があるので、この新しい小売の形態にはまだ対処すべき課題がある。

語彙リスト

☐ **1.**	transáction	名	商取引
☐ **2.**	stréamlìne 〜	動	〜を合理化する
☐ **3.**	pose 〜	動	(問題など)を引き起こす
☐ **4.**	sánitary	形	衛生的な
☐ **5.**	rétail style	名	小売の形態
☐ **6.**	íssues to addréss	熟	対処すべき問題

N O T E

解 答 例

In most states in the U.S., the age of adulthood is 18, but the MLDA is 21. Therefore, some people have called for lowering that age. Indeed, some African countries have the minimum drinking age of 18 or lower. However, people oppose a lower minimum drinking age because they believe it will have serious effects on the brain function of young people and cause an increase in traffic accidents.

(69 words)

アメリカの大半の州では成人年齢は18歳だが、最低飲酒年齢は21歳だ。そのため、その年齢の引き下げを要求する人がいる。実際、アフリカの一部の国では最低飲酒年齢は18歳、あるいはさらに低い。しかしながら、人々が最低飲酒年齢の引き下げに反対する理由は、それが若者の脳機能に重大な影響を及ぼし、交通事故の増加を引き起こすと考えているからである。

STEP 1
問題文の要点をつかむ

第1段落

The Minimum Legal Drinking Age (MLDA) is 21 in all 50 states in the United States, but 18 is the "age of majority" in 47 of the 50 states, allowing people to have the rights and responsibilities of an adult. Each state sets its own age of majority, which often coincides with the age at which one can vote, sign contracts, get married, and so on. Therefore, there have been a lot of discussions about whether setting the MLDA at 21 is fair and effective.

最低飲酒年齢（MLDA）は米国50州すべてで21歳だが、50州のうち47州では18歳が「成人年齢」であり、成人としての権利と責任を持つことが許される。各州が独自に成人年齢を定めており、多くの場合、選挙権、契約書への署名、結婚などができる年齢と一致している。そのため、最低飲酒年齢を21歳とすることが公正で効果的かどうかについては、これまで多くの議論がなされてきた。

語彙リスト

□ **1.**	age of majórity	熟	（法律用語）成人年齢
□ **2.**	còincíde with ～	熟	～と一致する
□ **3.**	sign a cóntract	熟	契約書に署名する

解説と要旨

　第1文は❶「アメリカの大半の州では成人年齢は18歳だ」、❷「最低飲酒年齢は21歳だ」の2つを要約に含める必要があります。第2文は「飲酒以外の結婚などの権利は18歳で得られる」ことが述べられていますが、語数制限を考えると、これを入れる余裕はないでしょう。❸「最低飲酒年齢を引き下げるべきかどうかが議論されている」は「最低飲酒年齢を引き下げるべきだという声もある」としても構いません。9点満点で、各区分3点として減点法で採点します。

[**要約例**] In most states in the U.S., the age of adulthood is 18, but the MLDA is 21. Therefore, some people have called for lowering that age.

「アメリカの大半の州では成人年齢は18歳だが、最低飲酒年齢は21歳だ。そのため、その年齢の引き下げを要求する人がいる」

[**注1**]「成人年齢」は (legal) age of adulthood のほか、adult age などとしてもよいだろう。

[**注2**]「～を要求する」は call for ～を用いる。

[**注3**]「～を引き下げる」は、lower 以外には reduce や decrease などでも可。

第2段落

As for African countries, the age at which people can buy alcohol is around 18 years old. However, in Ethiopia, people can buy alcohol at the age of 15, and in Zimbabwe at the age of 16. Algeria allows 18-year-olds to buy alcohol, but few shops sell it because it is a Muslim country.

アフリカ諸国に関しては、酒を購入できる年齢は18歳前後である。しかし、エチオピアでは15歳から、ジンバブエでは16歳から酒を買うことができる。アルジェリアは18歳から酒を買うことができるが、イスラム教国なので酒を売っている店はほとんどない。

語彙リスト

□ **4.**	as for ～	熟	～に関しては
□ **5.**	Múslim	形	イスラム教の

解説と要旨

第1文は、❶「アフリカ諸国では最低飲酒年齢は18前後だ」とします。第2文は❷「それよりさらに低い（国もある）」で十分です。エチオピアやジンバブエの例は、語数制限を考えると除外するしかないでしょう。8点満点で、各区分4点として減点法で採点します。

[**要約例**] Indeed, some African countries have the minimum drinking age of 18 or lower.

「実際、アフリカの一部の国では最低飲酒年齢は18歳、あるいはさらに低い」

第3段落

The main reasons for opposing the lowering of the drinking age in the U.S. are concerns that underage drinking may have serious effects on brain function and that increased underage drinking may lead to more traffic accidents and deaths.

　アメリカでの飲酒年齢の引き下げに反対する主な理由は、未成年者の飲酒が脳機能に深刻な影響を及ぼすかもしれないという懸念と、未成年者の飲酒が増えることで交通事故や死者が増えるかもしれないという懸念である。

語彙リスト

□ **6.**	oppóse ～	動	～に反対する
□ **7.**	lówer ～	動	～を引き下げる
□ **8.**	concérn	名	懸念
□ **9.**	ùnderáge drínking	名	未成年者の飲酒

解説と要旨

　文の骨格は❶「人々が最低飲酒年齢引き下げに反対する理由は、～だと考えているからである」です。具体的な理由は❷「若者の脳機能に重大な影響を及ぼす」、❸「それが交通事故の増加を引き起こす」です。「未成年者の飲酒が増え」の部分は常識の範囲なので、無視してもよいでしょう。8点満点で、各区分3点として減点法で採点します。0点になった場合、それ以上に減点はしません。

[**要約例**] However, people oppose a lower minimum drinking age because they believe it will have serious effects on the brain function of young people and cause an increase in traffic accidents.

　「しかしながら、人々が最低飲酒年齢の引き下げに反対する理由は、それが若者の脳機能に重大な影響を及ぼし、交通事故の増加を引き起こすと考えているからである」

準1級

04

[**モニター答案例1**]［6 / 25点］

In the United States, people are not allowed to drink alcohol until they are 21,

but they have the rights and responsibilities as adults at the age of 18 in most states.

✗ →though：－1点　　　　　　　　✗ →of：－2点

The gap has raised the debate about what age people can buy alcohol. In fact, in

✗ →a：－1点　　　　　　✗ →should be able to：－2点

Africa, even teenagers can buy alcohol. However, some people oppose lowering the

MLDA because there are many concerns. (66 words)

[**内容点**] 第1段落は❶❷❸ともOK。第2段落は❶❷共にヌケで－8点。第3段落は❷❸が共に不十分で、－5点。前半で語数を使いすぎた結果、後半が不十分な内容となってしまっている。以上、－13点。

[**文法点**] －6点。「大半の州では18歳で大人の権利と責任を有する」の部分は主張ではなく譲歩なので、butはthoughに代える必要がある。「どの年齢で酒を買うことができるかについての議論」は、世界中で数多くなされているはずなので特定できない。よって the debate はa debate とする。

[**総評**] 各段落の語数のバランスを考えないと、このように後半が不十分になる。

[**モニター答案例2**]［6 / 25点］

The Minimum Legal Drinking Age is different from the age of majority ✗.

✗ →higher than：内容点で減点　　ヌケ→ in the U.S.：内容点で減点

Many people discuss whether setting the MLDA at 21 is fair and effective. In some

African countries, the age at which people can buy alcohol is around 18 years old.

The main reason for opposition to lowering the MLDA is that people ✗concerned

✗ ヌケ→are：－2点

about bad effect such ✕ increase in traffic accidents and death or ✕ rise in underage

✕ →effects：−1点　　ヌケ→as an：−2点　　✕ →deaths：−1点　　✕ ヌケ→a：−1点

drinking.

(70 words)

［**内容点**］第1段落の❶❷が不十分。−5点。❸はOK。第2段落は❶はOKだが、❷のヌケで−4点。第3段落の❶はOK。❷がヌケで−3点。❸はOK。以上、−12点。

［**文法点**］−7点。

［**総評**］抽象名詞（effect、increase、death など）を使っていいのは、その単語が可算名詞か不可算名詞なのか、動詞とのコロケーションはどうか、などの知識がある場合だけである。そのあたりを適当に「たぶんこうかな？」という思いで書いているうちは高得点は望めないだろう。これは要約問題に限らず、英作文問題全般に言えることである。

STEP3
ネイティブスピーカーの解答に学ぶ

模範解答

Although one must be 21 to drink in the US, in the majority of states the age of legal adulthood is 18. This disparity is a reason behind calls to lower the drinking age to match it. As a point of contrast, most African nations permit individuals to buy alcohol from age 18. Concerns about adverse health effects and accidents seem to be the main obstacle to changing this law.

(70 words)

米国では飲酒するためには21歳になっていないといけないが、大半の州では成人年齢は18歳である。この差が、成人年齢に合わせるために飲酒年齢を引き下げることを求める声の背景にある理由である。対照的な点として、たいていのアフリカの国では18歳から個人がお酒を買うことを許可している。健康への悪影響や事故への懸念が、この法律を変えることに対する主な障害となっているようだ。

語彙リスト

□ **1.**	dispárity	名	相違、格差
□ **2.**	call to (V)	熟	(V) への要請
□ **3.**	as a point of cóntrast	熟	対照的な点として
□ **4.**	advérse health effècts	名	健康への悪影響　＊adverseのアクセントは複数ある。

N O T E

解 答 例

Clothing rental subscriptions are becoming increasingly popular in the United States. For a monthly fee, you can select your favorite items or have a stylist coordinate your outfits. This service is inexpensive and environmentally friendly because it reduces the amount of clothing that would normally be disposed of after one use. The downsides are that you cannot touch or try on such items, and most of them are not new.

(70 words)

アメリカでは、洋服レンタルのサブスクリプションの人気がますます高まっている。月額料金で好きなアイテムを選択したり、スタイリストに服をコーディネートしてもらったりすることができる。このサービスは安価で環境によい。なぜならそれによって通常なら一度着て処分されてしまうような服の量を減らせるからだ。問題点は、そうした商品を触ることも試着することもできないことと、その大半が新品ではないということだ。

STEP 1
問題文の要点をつかむ

第1段落

Clothing rental subscription is a service that allows you to rent various items for a monthly fee. There are different rental methods depending on the number of items delivered, and there are plans where you can choose your favorite items, and plans where you receive coordinated outfits selected by a stylist. In the United States, as of 2020, over 11 million users have used this service. And the US clothing rental market could reach $4.4 billion by 2028.

洋服レンタルのサブスクリプションは、月額料金でさまざまなアイテムをレンタルできるサービスだ。届くアイテム数によってレンタル方法が異なり、好きなアイテムを選べるプランや、スタイリストが選んだコーディネートされた服が届くプランなどがある。米国では2020年の時点で、1,100万人以上がこのサービスを利用した。また、米国の衣料品レンタル市場は2028年までに44億ドルに達するかもしれない。

語彙リスト

☐ 1.	subscríption	图	サブスクリプション、定額サービス
☐ 2.	mónthly fee	图	月ごとの支払い
☐ 3.	coórdinate ~	動	（服・家具など）をコーディネートする
☐ 4.	óutfit	图	衣服 ※トータルで魅力的に見える一式の服。
☐ 5.	as of ~	熟	～現在で、～の時点で

解説と要旨

第1段落の主張は、第3～4文にある❶「アメリカでは洋服レンタルのサブスクリプションの人気が高まっている」で、これを要約に含める必要があります。ただし、具体的数字は語数制限を考えれば入れなくてもよいでしょう。サービスの内容を説明し

た第1文は、❷「月額料金で好きなアイテムを選べる」とします。第2文を考慮して「好きな」は「多くの」「さまざまな」でもよいでしょう。第2文にある❸「スタイリストに服をコーディネートしてもらえる」という情報は必要です。9点満点で、各区分3点として減点法で採点します。

[要約例] Clothing rental subscriptions are becoming increasingly popular in the United States. For a monthly fee, you can select your favorite items or have a stylist coordinate your outfits.

「アメリカでは、洋服レンタルのサブスクリプションの人気がますます高まっている。月額料金で好きなアイテムを選択したり、スタイリストに服をコーディネートしてもらったりすることができる」

[注1]「～を選択する」は、choose ～、select ～以外に、rent ～「(お金を出して) ～を借りる」も可。wear ～「～を身につけている」は不可。

[注2]「月額で」は、if you pay a (fixed) monthly fee などと書くこともできる。

[注3]「スタイリストに服をコーディネートしてもらう」は、have a stylist coordinate your outfits が直訳だが、have a stylist select your outfits とすることもできる。

[注4] この文の「服」は「トータルで魅力的に見える一式の服」の意味なのでoutfits が適切。不可算名詞の attire も可。

第2段落

With a subscription service, you can rent unique designer items for a low price. This cuts down on the number of items you buy and wear only once and throw away. The amount of clothing waste in Japan alone exceeds 500,000 tons annually, so such a service would be beneficial to the environment.

サブスクリプションサービスを利用すれば、ユニークなブランド品を低価格でレンタルできる。これによって、買って一度だけ着て捨てるアイテムの数を減らすことができる。日本だけでも衣料品の廃棄量は年間50万トンを超えており、このようなサービスは環境にも有益だろう。

語彙リスト

□ 6.	designer item	名	ブランド品
□ 7.	cut down on ～	熟	(必要に迫られて) ～を切り詰める、減らす
□ 8.	waste	名	廃棄物
□ 9.	exceed ～	動	～を超える

　第1文は❶「このサービスは安価である」とまとめます。save money「お金の節約になる」などでもよいでしょう。第2文は❷「通常なら一度着て捨ててしまうような服」、第3文は❸「（服の）廃棄量を減らせるので環境によい」とそれぞれまとめます。❷は仮定法になることに注意したいところです。8点満点で、各区分3点として減点法で採点します。0点になった場合、それ以上には減点しません。

[**要約例**] This service is inexpensive and environmentally friendly because it reduces the amount of clothing that would normally be disposed of after one use.

　「このサービスは安価で環境によい。なぜならそれによって通常なら一度着て処分されてしまうような服の量を減らせるからだ」

[**注1**]「一度着て処分されてしまうような服の量を減らせる」は、「〜によって服を無駄にすることをなくせる」と考え、〜 prevent you from wasting clothes とすることもできる。

[**注2**]「一度着て捨てる」は、be disposed [discarded / thrown away] after one [minimal / a single] use などが適切。

[**注3**]「環境によい」はgood for the environment、environmentally friendly、eco-friendly など。

第3段落

　On the other hand, the disadvantage of a clothing rental subscription is that you cannot try the items on in advance. Nor can you pick up the actual item and touch it. You can only check the images and information posted, and there may be some discrepancies. Moreover, most of the products handled by the clothing subscription service are not new.

　一方、洋服レンタルのサブスクリプションのデメリットは、事前に服を試着できないことだ。実物を手に取って触ることもできない。掲載されている画像や情報でしか確認できないため、多少の食い違いが生じることもある。しかも、洋服のサブスクリプションで扱われる商品のほとんどが新品ではない。

□	**10.**	try ～ on / try on ～	熟 ～を試着する
□	**11.**	in advánce	熟 あらかじめ
□	**12.**	pick ～ up / pick up ～	熟 ～を手に取る
□	**13.**	discrépancy	名 相違、ズレ

解説と要旨

　第1文は❶「そうした商品を試着できない」とします。第2文は❷「そうした商品を触ることができない」とします。ここを you do not know what they look like「実物がどんなものかわからない」、the clothes you rent may be different from what you expected「借りた服が、思っていたものとは異なるかもしれない」などとすることもできます。第3文は省いても問題ないでしょう。第4文は❸「そうした商品の大半が新品ではない」とまとめればよいでしょう。8点満点で、各区分3点として減点法で採点します。0点になった場合、それ以上には減点しません。

［要約例］The downsides are that you cannot touch or try on such items, and most of them are not new.

　「問題点は、そうした商品を触ることも試着することもできないことと、その大半が新品ではないということだ」

［注1］「問題点は ～ だ」、は the disadvantage [problem] is that SV や on the downside, SV などと書くこともできる。

［注2］語数に余裕があれば before you order them「それらを注文する前に」を入れておきたい。

STEP 2
モニター答案でポイントをつかむ

［モニター答案例1］［3 / 25点］

　These days, more and more people are using clothing rental subscription. This

is a service by which you can rent various clothing items just by paying a low monthly fee. This <u>subscription</u> service can decrease the number of clothing items

✕ →トル：−1点

thrown away after being used only once, which <u>does good to</u> the environment.

✕ →is good for：内容点で減点

However, this service is not necessarily a perfect one, because you <u>have to check</u>

✕ →cannot see or try on the actual items：内容点で減点

<u>items only on the Internet or these items</u> are usually secondhand.　　　(78 words)

✕ →and：−2点　✕ →they：−1点

［**内容点**］語数制限を8語オーバーしているので−8点。第1段落は❶❷はOKだが、❸がヌケで−3点。第2段落の❶は、第2文のa low monthly feeに含まれているので可とする。❷は可とする。❸は語の選択を間違っているので−3点。第3段落の❶❷は不十分で、表現に問題があるので、−4点。❸はOK。以上、−18点。

［**文法点**］−4点。do good to 〜は「〜に（直接）有用な影響を与える」の意味。このサービスは間接的に環境によいだけなので不自然。

［**総評**］文法はまずまずだが、内容面の記述が正確ではない。もう少し英文の主張を吟味した上で答えを書くこと。

［**モニター答案例2**］［**11 / 25点**］

Clothing rental subscription is a service that enables you to rent many kinds of

items if you pay a monthly fee. The service is popular in the US. It helps you save

<u>much</u> money and will reduce the amount of clothing waste. However, you cannot

✕ →トル：−1点

try the items on in advance. In addition, most of the products handled by the service

are used items.　　　　　　　　　　　　　　　　　　　　　　(64 words)

［**内容点**］第1段落は❶❷ともOKだが、余分な情報を入れたために❸がヌケで−3点。第2段落の❶はOKだが、❷がヌケで−3点。❸は「環境によい」の部分がヌケで−1点。第3段落の❶は本文を8語連続で写しているので不可で−3点。❷がヌケで−3点。❸はOK。以上、−13点。

［**文法点**］−1点。muchは非常に堅い文を除いて、肯定文では使えない。また「多くのお金の節約」になるかどうかは本文からはわからない。

［**総評**］本文の内容を「内容を変えずにいかに自分の言葉で言い換えられるか」が採点ポイントなので、本文を8語もそのまま引用すれば点数を引かれてしまう。

STEP 3
ネイティブスピーカーの解答に学ぶ

Clothing rental services, which are a growing market in the United States, offer a variety of options for consumers to borrow luxury items. Such services can be considered eco-friendly, since they reduce the amount of clothing which is discarded after minimal use, and so are well-suited to Japan. However, there are some drawbacks for customers, including not being able to touch or try on the items before they order them.

(70 words)

米国で成長市場となっている洋服のレンタルサービスは、消費者が高級品を借りるためのさまざまな選択肢を提供している。このようなサービスは、最小限の使用の後で廃棄される衣類の量を減らすため、環境に優しいと考えることができ、日本にも適している。しかし、顧客にとっては、注文する前に商品に触ったり、試着したりすることができないなどの欠点もある。

語 彙 リ ス ト

☐ **1.**	a varíety of ～	熟	さまざまな～
☐ **2.**	discárd ～	動	～を捨てる

解答例

An AI chatbot is a service that has greatly improved marketing campaign performances. Chatbots are always available and can answer questions instantly. They can communicate in real time, asking questions to fine-tune the service to a customer's demands. However, they cannot respond to long, difficult questions or understand people's feelings, which could damage a brand's reputation. Customers will need to contact humans when AI communication breaks down.

(67 words)

AIチャットボットは、マーケティングキャンペーンのパフォーマンスを大きく向上させたサービスだ。チャットボットはいつでも利用可能で、質問に即座に答えることができる。それらはリアルタイムでやりとりができ、いくつかの質問をすることで、顧客の要求に合わせてサービスを微調整することができる。しかし、長くて難しい質問に答えることはできないし、人々の気持ちを理解できないことで、ブランドの評判を落としかねない。顧客は、AIとのやりとりが機能しなくなったときに人間に連絡する必要があるだろう。

STEP 1
問題文の要点をつかむ

第1段落

An AI chatbot is a service that uses AI machine learning to automatically present appropriate answers to chat questions. The introduction of AI chatbots in marketing has helped greatly improve campaign performances. This market is expected to grow from $2.6 billion in 2019 to $9.4 billion by 2024.

AIチャットボットとは、AIの機械学習を利用して、チャットの質問に対して適切な回答を自動的に提示するサービスのことだ。AIチャットボットをマーケティングに導入することで、キャンペーンの実績の大きな向上に役立っている。この市場は2019年の26億ドルから2024年には94億ドルに成長すると予想されている。

語彙リスト

□ **1.** presént 〜　　　　　　　　　　　動 〜を提示する
□ **2.** campáign perfórmance　　　　名 キャンペーンの実績

解説と要旨

第1文はAIチャットボットの説明ですが、これを答えに含める語数の余裕はありません。第2文の❶「AIチャットボットは〜なサービスだ」、❷「マーケティングキャンペーンのパフォーマンスを大きく向上させた」はこの文の主張なので外せません。第3文は要約文に入れる必要はないでしょう。8点満点で、各区分4点として減点法で採点します。

［**要　約　例**］An AI chatbot is a service that has greatly improved marketing campaign performances.

「AIチャットボットは、マーケティングキャンペーンのパフォーマンスを大きく向上させたサービスだ」

［**注1**］AI chatbot は可算名詞であることに注意すること。

[注2]「マーケティングキャンペーンのパフォーマンスを大きく向上させた」は、「マーケティングにおいて絶大なる効果を発揮する道具」an immensely powerful tool in marketing、「～はマーケティングにおいて極めて重要な役割を果たしている」play a crucial role in marketing などとしてもよいだろう。単に be used in marketing では不十分。

第2段落

Chatbots are available 24/7 and can respond instantly to questions from customers. They can also communicate with website visitors and social media followers in real-time. Additionally, they can be used to ask questions about customer preferences and adjust the service to the customer's needs accordingly.

チャットボットは毎日24時間利用可能で、顧客からの質問に即座に対応できる。また、ウェブサイトの訪問者やソーシャルメディアのフォロワーとリアルタイムでやりとりすることもできる。さらに、顧客の好みについて質問し、それに応じてサービスを顧客のニーズに合わせて調整するために使用することもできる。

語彙リスト

□			
3.	24/7	副	24時間年中無休で、いつも ※ twenty-four seven と発音する。
4.	ínstantly	副	すぐに
5.	additíonally	副	加えて
6.	adjúst A to B	熟	AをBに合わせる

解説と要旨

第1文は❶「24時間年中無休で、即座に質問に答えることができる」とします。第2文は❷「リアルタイムでやりとりができる」とします。「ウェブサイトの訪問者やソーシャルメディアのフォロワー」は後で「顧客」としてまとめれば十分でしょう。第3文は❸「いくつかの質問をすることで、顧客のニーズに合わせてサービスを調整することができる」とします。9点満点で、各区分3点として減点法で採点します。

[要約文] Chatbots are always available and can answer questions instantly. They can communicate in real time, asking questions to fine-tune the service to a customer's demands.

「チャットボットはいつでも利用可能で、質問に即座に答えることができる。それらはリアルタイムで意思の疎通ができ、いくつかの質問をすることで、顧客の要求に合わせてサービスを微調整することができる」

[注1]「24時間年中無休で」は、本文には24/7とあるので、be always available、whenever you want to ask questions などに言い換える。

[注2]「即座に」は、immediately、instantly、right away、straight away など。soon「今から短時間で」ではない。

[注3]「〜の要求に合わせる」は、meet one's demands [needs] など。

[注4]「(サービス) を調整する」は、「〜を微調整する」という意味のfine-tuneを用いる。本文のadjustを借用しても可。

第3段落

However, as a drawback, chatbots cannot grasp the user's emotions. In fact, they may not be possible to understand how the user they are chatting with is feeling. This can make the chatbot appear emotionally insensitive and damage the brand's reputation. In addition, it is difficult to respond to long questions that even humans find difficult to answer. When communication breaks down, it is necessary to devise ways for the customer to talk with human staff, such as connecting the customer to a call center.

しかし、欠点の一つとして、チャットボットはユーザーの感情を把握することができないことがあげられる。実際、チャットの相手であるユーザーがどのように感じているかを理解することはできないかもしれない。このためチャットボットが感情的に無神経に見え、ブランドの評判を落とす可能性があるのだ。また、人間でも答えにくいような長い質問には対応しにくい。やりとりが機能しなくなった場合、コールセンターにつなぐなど、顧客が人間のスタッフと話せるやり方を考案することが必要だ。

06

語彙リスト

□ **7.**	dráwbàck	图	欠点
□ **8.**	grasp 〜	動	〜を把握する
□ **9.**	insénsitive	形	鈍感な、無神経な
□ **10.**	rèputátion	图	評判
□ **11.**	devíse 〜	動	〜を考案する

　第1～3文は❶「ユーザーの気持ちを理解できないことで、ブランドの評判を落としかねない」とします。第4文は❷「長くて難しい質問に答えたりすることはできない」でよいでしょう。第5文は❸「顧客は、AIとのやりとりが機能しなくなったときに人間に連絡する必要があるだろう」とします。8点満点で、各区分3点として減点法で採点します。0点となった場合、それ以上の減点はしません。

[要約例] However, they cannot respond to long, difficult questions or understand people's feelings, which could damage a brand's reputation. Customers will need to contact humans when AI communication breaks down.

　「しかし、長くて難しい質問に答えることはできないし、人々の気持ちを理解できないことで、ブランドの評判を落としかねない。顧客は、AIとのやりとりが機能しなくなったときに人間に連絡する必要があるだろう。」

[注1]「～の気持ち」は、one's feelings と複数形にすることに注意。how one feels とすることもできる。

[注2]「～の評判を落とす」は、damage [ruin / bring down / lower] one's reputation。

STEP2
モニター答案でポイントをつかむ

［モニター答案例1］［6 / 25点］

　An AI Chatbot is a service that <u>answer</u> your questions appropriately by using
　　　　　　　　　　　　　　　　✕ →answers：−1点
AI machine learning. You can use Chatbots whenever you want. You can use them

to ask questions about customer preferences and adjust the service to the

customer's needs accordingly. However, they cannot understand <u>user's</u> feelings.
　　　　　　　　　　　　　　　　　　　　　　　　　　　　ヌケ→a：−1点
Also, it is hard for them to answer to long questions that even <u>human</u> struggle to
　　　　　　　　　　　　　　　　　　　　　　　　　　✕ →humans：−1点
answer.　　　　　　　　　　　　　　　　　　　　　　　　　　　　(65 words)

［**内容点**］第1段落の❶はOKだが、余分な情報を入れたために❷がヌケで−4点。第2段落の❶は不十分。「即座に答えてくれる」がないので−1点。❷はヌケで−3点。❸は本文を14語連続で写しているので不可で−3点。第3段落は❶が不十分で「ブランドの評判を落としかねない」がないので−2点。❷はOK。❸はヌケで−3点。以上、−16点。

［**文法点**］−3点。関係代名詞の先行詞が単数形なら、関係代名詞節内の動詞もそれに呼応する。

［**総評**］名詞を書くときには、当然のことだが、冠詞の有無、単複などを常に意識すること。

［**モニター答案例2**］［**0 / 25点**］

An AI Chatbot is a system that uses AI machine that give you appropriate
✗ →gives you appropriate answers：−4点
answer to questions, which has a good influence on economy. By using this, you can
✗ ヌケ→ the：−1点
get answers to your questions instantly, communicate with others in real time on the
✗ → It can answer your questions：語数調整：減点なし
Internet, and adjust them to your needs. However, since they have difficulty
✗ →the service：内容面で減点
understanding people's emotion and responding ✗ questions that is too long to
✗ →emotions：−1点   ヌケ→ to：−1点   ✗ →are：−1点
answer, we should find ways of talking with others in case communication breaks

down.   (80 words)

［**内容点**］そもそも語数を10 words オーバーしているので、−10点。第1段落の❶はOK。❷がヌケで−4点。第2段落の❶は不十分で−2点。❷はOK。❸は adjust them が adjust the service の間違いだし説明が不十分。−2点。第3段落の❶が不十分で−2点。❷はOK。❸はOK。以上、−20点。

［**文法点**］−8点。

［**総評**］語数制限を守っていないものにまともな答案が少ない気がする。これは、「決まりを守る」という感覚が欠落していて、それが英作文にも出ているからであろう。

STEP 3
ネイティブスピーカーの解答に学ぶ

模範解答

AI chatbots, which utilize machine learning, offer instant responses to customer queries, and have significantly improved marketing. They are always available, engage with customers through online media, and collect data in order to customize services. However, a major drawback is their inability to understand user emotions, potentially leading to perceived insensitivity and harm to brand reputation. For complex or emotionally charged queries, connecting customers to a human operator is recommended. (70 words)

機械学習を活用した AI チャットボットは、顧客からの問い合わせに即座に対応し、マーケティングを大幅に改善した。それらは常に利用可能で、オンラインメディアを通じて顧客と関わり、サービスをカスタマイズするためにデータを収集する。しかし、大きな欠点の一つは、ユーザーの感情を理解できないことであり、無神経であると認識されたり、ブランドの評判を傷つける可能性がある。複雑な、あるいは感情的な問い合わせには、人間のオペレーターにつなぐことが推奨される。

語彙リスト

☐ **1.**	quéry	名	問い合わせ
☐ **2.**	significantly	副	（数量が）かなり
☐ **3.**	engáge with ～	熟	～と関わる
☐ **4.**	cústomize ～	動	～をカスタマイズする
☐ **5.**	insènsitívity	名	無神経、鈍感
☐ **6.**	emótionally chàrged	熟	感情がからんだ

N O T E

解答例

A thrift shop is a type of retail store that sells donated goods and gives the profit to charities. These shops are operated by charitable organizations and their workers are volunteers. The U.S. currently has about 30,000 such outlets. Shopping at these shops is cost-effective and helps protect the environment. However, the problem is that products purchased at thrift shops do not come with a warranty.

(66 words)

スリフトショップとは、寄付された品物を販売して、その収益を慈善団体に寄付する小売店の一形態である。これらの店は慈善団体により運営され、スタッフもボランティアである。現在、アメリカにはそのような店がおよそ 30,000 店ある。こうした店での買い物は、経済的で、また環境保護に貢献できる。しかし、問題点は、スリフトショップで購入した商品には保証が付かないことである。

STEP 1
問題文の要点をつかむ

第1段落

A thrift shop is a form of retail store where used clothes, furniture, home appliances, etc, are collected through donations and resold, with the proceeds donated to charitable activities. There were about 30,000 thrift shops in the US in 2023. Generally, the shops are primarily run by charitable organizations and staffed by volunteers. Therefore, whether you donate, buy, or work in the shop, everyone involved contributes to charity.

スリフトショップとは、中古の衣料品や家具、家電製品などを寄付によって集め、再販売し、その収益を慈善活動に寄付する小売店の一形態である。2023年の時点で、アメリカには約30,000店のスリフトショップがある。一般的に、これらの店は主に慈善団体によって運営され、スタッフもボランティアによって賄われている。そのため、寄付をするにしても、購入するにしても、ショップで働くにしても、関係者全員がチャリティーに貢献していることになる。

語彙リスト

☐ 1.	thrift	名	倹約
☐ 2.	rétail store	名	小売店
☐ 3.	home appliance	名	家電製品
☐ 4.	donátion	名	寄付
☐ 5.	próceeds	名	(販売、取引などの) 売上高
☐ 6.	donáte ～	動	～を寄付する　※ (米) では dónate
☐ 7.	be staffed	熟	スタッフとして働く

解説と要旨

　第1文は、❶「スリフトショップは、寄付された品物を販売する」、❷「その収益は慈善団体に寄付される」とします。第3〜4文は❸「慈善団体により運営され、スタッ

フもボランティアである」とすれば十分です。第1段落のまとめとして最後に、第2文の内容の❹「現在アメリカにはおよそ30,000店のそのような店がある」を入れるとよいでしょう。10点満点で、各区分3点として減点法で採点します。0点になった場合、それ以上減点しません。

[要約文] A thrift shop is a type of retail store that sells donated goods and gives the profit to charities. These shops are operated by charitable organizations and their workers are volunteers. The U.S. currently has about 30,000 such outlets.

「スリフトショップとは、寄付された品物を販売して、その収益を慈善団体に寄付する小売店の一形態である。これらの店は慈善団体により運営され、スタッフもボランティアである。現在、アメリカにはそのような店がおよそ30,000店ある」

[注1] 本文では are collected through donations, and resold となっているが、sell donated items ぐらいに言い換えたい。

[注2] 「慈善団体」に charity を使う場合、「慈善事業」の意味では不可算名詞だが、「(個々の)慈善団体」の意味では可算名詞の扱いとなる。ここではいずれも可である。

[注3] 「スタッフもボランティアである」は、be operated by unpaid staff と書くこともできる。staff という語は「スタッフ全員」を表すので staffs とはしないこと。

[注4] 最終文は There are currently 30,000 such stores in the U.S. と書くこともできる。

第2段落

Thrift shops are filled with a wide variety of clothing styles, furniture and homewares. You can save a large amount of money by shopping there because everything is reasonably priced. More importantly, the more you use thrift shops, the more you help save the environment.

スリフトショップは、幅広いスタイルの衣服、家具、家庭用品であふれている。あらゆるものが手頃な価格なので、そこで買い物をすれば、かなりの節約になる。さらに重要なことに、スリフトショップを利用すればするほど、環境保護に貢献することになるのだ。

語彙リスト

☐ 8.	be filled with 〜	熟	〜で満たされている
☐ 9.	a wide variety of 〜	熟	幅広い〜

☐ **10.**	hómewàre	名	家庭用品
☐ **11.**	more impórtantly	熟	さらに重要なことに

第1～2文は、**❶**「スリフトショップで買い物すれば、経済的である」とします。第3文は**❷**「環境保護に役立つ」としておけばよいでしょう。8点満点で、各区分4点として減点法で採点します。

[**要約文**] Shopping at these shops is cost-effective and helps protect the environment.
「こうした店での買い物は、経済的で、また環境保護に貢献できる」

[**注1**] 語数を気にしなければShopping at these shops is a wise way to save your money. などと書くこともできる。

[**注2**]「経済的な」はcost-effective とする。

[**注3**]「環境保護に貢献できる」は、contribute to the protection of the environment とか、help protect the environment とする。protect はsave や conserve などでも可。

[**注4**]「地球の自然環境」の意味では environment に the をつけることに注意。

第 3 段 落

Despite these advantages, there are some drawbacks. As is the case with secondhand stores in general, no warranty is provided for anything purchased at a thrift shop. For example, a thrift shop stereo could last a lifetime, or it could break in a day. The one-year warranty you usually get when you buy from a retail store is not included with items bought at a thrift shop.

こうした利点がある反面、いくつか欠点もある。中古品店全般に言えることだが、スリフトショップで購入したいかなるものにも保証がない。例えば、スリフトショップのステレオは一生使えるかもしれないし、1日で壊れてしまうかもしれない。通常、小売店で購入した場合についてくる1年間の保証は、スリフトショップで購入したものにはついていない。

☐ **12.**	despíte ～	前	～にもかかわらず
☐ **13.**	dráwbàck	名	欠点
☐ **14.**	as is the case with ～	熟	～にはよくあることだが

□ **15.**	last a lífetìme	熟	生涯の間持つ、一生使える
□ **16.**	wárranty	名	保証 (書)

　第3段落の主張は第2文にあります。第2文と第4文はほぼ同様のことを言っていますが、第2文は中古品店全般について、第4文はスリフトショップについて、どちらも購入商品に保証がないことを問題点としてあげています。よって、「問題点は、スリフトショップで購入した商品は保証がないことである」とまとめれば十分です。第3文はこれの具体例なのでなくてもいいでしょう。もし書くならば、たとえば「買ったものは次の日に壊れる可能性があり、その場合でも返金してもらえない (What you buy could break the next day, and even then you cannot get a refund.)」となりますが、これでは語数オーバーになってしまいます。7点満点で、減点法で採点します。

[要約文] However, the problem is that products purchased at thrift shops do not come with a warranty.

　「しかし問題点は、スリフトショップで購入した商品には保証が付かないことである」
[注1]「スリフトショップで購入した商品」は、特定できないので the をつけないこと。
[注2]「スリフトショップ」は、一般論なので複数形にすること。

STEP 2
モニター答案でポイントをつかむ

[モニター答案例1] [15 / 25点]

　In a thrift shop, there are various kinds of used items like clothes. Generally, that shop is mainly run by ✕ charity, which means everyone who is involved in that
　　　　　　　　　　　　　　　ヌケ→a : -1点
shop contributes to charity. If you do shopping there, you can not only save <u>much</u>
　　　　　　　　　　　　　　　　　　　　　　　　　　　　　✕ →a lot of : -1点
money but also preserve the environment. However, one disadvantage is that there

is no warranty on anything at a thrift shop.　　　　　　　　　　　　　　(65 words)

［**内容点**］第1段落の❶は、「寄付された品物を販売する」がなく不十分で－2点。❷はヌケで－3点。❸は可とする。❹ヌケで－3点。第2段落は❶❷ともにOK。第3段落はOK。以上、－8点。

［**文法点**］－2点。最初に使われているcharityは「慈善団体」の意味なので可算名詞の扱いとなる。2つ目のcharityは不可算名詞でOK。muchは、非常に堅い文以外では、疑問文や否定文でしか使われない。

［**総評**］さらに上級者になりたければ、言葉を切り詰めることによって、情報をぎゅっと入れる訓練をすること。

［**モニター答案例2**］［**14 / 25点**］

A thrift shop is a form of retail store where used items are collected through donations and resold. They are primarily run by charitable organizations. You can buy cheap things and help save the environment. However, there is no warranty on anything you purchase at a thrift shop. Those things could break in a day because

it has been used for some time.　　　　　　　　　　　　　　　　　(63 words)

✘ →they have：－1点

［**内容点**］第1段落❶❸は、ほぼ本文の丸写しなので点はない。－6点。❷❹は書かれていない。－4点。以上から、この段落は－10点とする。第2段落の❶❷は共にOK。第3段落はOK。以上、－10点。

［**文法点**］－1点。

［**総評**］「英語要約は、該当箇所を見つけて、それを引用する」という間違った考えをもっているようだが、この問題は「英作文の力」を評価するための問題である。何とか苦労して言い換える訓練をしよう。

模範解答

Thrift shops operate as retail stores which sell donated and second-hand items, including clothes and furniture. Run by volunteers, these shops offer diverse goods at low prices, and profits fund the charitable activities of the managing organization. However, one limitation of these stores is that purchases do not include regular warranties. Despite this, thrift shops give consumers the opportunity to contribute to charity while enjoying affordable and eco-friendly shopping.

(69 words)

スリフトショップは、衣類や家具など、寄付された中古品を販売する小売店として運営されている。これらの店はボランティアによって運営され、多様な商品を低価格で提供し、その利益を運営団体の慈善活動に充てている。しかし、これらの店の限界の一つは、購入品に通常の保証が含まれていないことである。こうしたことにもかかわらず、スリフトショップは消費者に、手頃な価格で環境に優しい買い物を楽しみながら、慈善活動に貢献する機会を与えてくれる。

語彙リスト

☐ **1.**	sécond-hánd	形 中古の	（used の曖昧性を避けるためおすすめ）
☐ **2.**	fund 〜	動 〜に資金を提供する	
☐ **3.**	affórdable	形 手頃な	

N O T E

解答例

Thermal recycling is a method of recovering and reusing the heat generated when waste is burned that could not be otherwise recycled. More than half of Japan's waste plastic was processed in this way in 2022. This kind of recycling can suppress the generation of global-warming inducing methane gas, which is produced when plastics degrade. On the downside, thermal recycling emits toxic substances such as dioxin and carbon dioxide.

(69 words)

サーマルリサイクルとは、他のやり方ではリサイクルできない廃棄物を燃やした際に発生する熱を回収し、再利用するやり方である。2022年には日本の廃プラスチックの半分以上がこの方法で処理された。プラスチックが劣化した時に生み出される地球温暖化を誘発するメタンガスの発生を、この種のリサイクルは抑えることができる。よくない面としては、サーマルリサイクルによってダイオキシンなどの有毒物質および二酸化炭素が発生するということだ。

STEP 1
問題文の要点をつかむ

第1段落

Certain forms of recycling can be used on certain types of waste. These include material recycling, which reuses waste as raw materials for new products, and chemical recycling, which converts waste into other substances through chemical synthesis and uses those substances as raw materials to create new products. However, some materials cannot be recycled in these ways. Instead, these materials undergo thermal recycling, which is a method that recovers and utilizes the heat generated when burning waste. When these materials are burned, the energy created is called "thermal energy." According to the Ministry of Economy, Trade and Industry, 63% of the total waste plastic discarded in Japan in 2022 was processed by means of thermal recycling.

リサイクルには、廃棄物のある種類によって利用できるある形態がある。廃棄物を新たな製品の原料として再利用するマテリアルリサイクルや、廃棄物を化学合成によって別の物質に変え、その物質を原料として新たな製品を作るケミカルリサイクルなどである。しかし、これらの方法でリサイクルできない素材もある。それに代わり、こうした素材には、廃棄物を燃やすときに発生する熱を回収・利用する方法であるサーマルリサイクルが行われる。こうした素材を燃やしたときに発生するエネルギーを「サーマルエネルギー」という。経済産業省によると、2022年に日本で廃棄された廃プラスチック全体の63%がサーマルリサイクルによって処理された。

語彙リスト

□ 1.	waste	名	廃棄物
□ 2.	convért A into B	熟	AをBに変換する
□ 3.	chémical sýnthesis	名	化学合成
□ 4.	súbstance	名	物質
□ 5.	thérmal	形	熱の

準1級

08

☐ **6.**	útilize 〜	動	〜を利用する
☐ **7.**	génerate 〜	動	〜を生み出す
☐ **8.**	the Mínistry of Ecónomy, Trade, and Índustry	名	経済産業省
☐ **9.**	prócess 〜	動	〜を処理する

解説と要旨

　第1段落は、リサイクルの方法についての概略を述べたあと、However で始まる第3文以降でサーマルリサイクルの話題が導入されています。第2、第3段落で、このサーマルリサイクルの話題が展開されていることから、第1段落の第4文、第5文の内容を❶「サーマルリサイクルとは、〜を燃やすことで生み出される熱を回収し再利用するやり方である」として主題に据えるのがよいでしょう。第1、第2文で示された具体的なリサイクルの方法は省略して、❷「他の方法ではリサイクルできない廃棄物」とすれば十分です。最終文は❸「2022年には日本の廃プラスチックの63%がサーマルリサイクルで処理された」とすればよいでしょう。9点満点で、各区分3点として減点法で採点します。

[**要約例**] Thermal recycling is a method of recovering and reusing the heat generated when waste is burned that could not be otherwise recycled. More than half of Japan's waste plastic was processed in this way in 2022.

　「サーマルリサイクルとは、他のやり方ではリサイクルできない廃棄物を燃やした際に発生する熱を回収し、再利用するやり方である。2022年には日本の廃プラスチックの半分以上がこの方法で処理された」

[**注1**] この文での「〜のやり方」は、「1つの確立された方法」なので method が最適。注意すべきは method は、method for [of] (V)ing、method ＋関係代名詞節は可だが、method to (V) とは言わないということである。

[**注2**] 「他のやり方ではリサイクルできない廃棄物」は、「たとえもしリサイクルしようとしても他の方法ではリサイクルできない廃棄物」の意味なので仮定法が適切である。

第2段落

　This is beneficial because when plastic breaks down, it generates methane gas, one of the greenhouse gases that promote global warming. Methane gas is said to have a greenhouse effect more than 20 times that of carbon dioxide. Thermal recycling can suppress the generation of methane gas that accompanies the deterioration of plastics.

　これが効果的なのは、プラスチックが分解される際に、地球温暖化を促進する温室効果ガスのひとつであるメタンガスが発生するからだ。メタンガスは二酸化炭素の20倍以上の温室効果があると言われている。サーマルリサイクルは、プラスチックの劣化に伴うメタンガスの発生を抑制することができる。

解説と要旨

　第1～2文は❶「プラスチックが劣化した時に、地球温暖化を誘発するメタンガスが発生する」とし、第3文は❷「サーマルリサイクルは、メタンガスの発生を抑えることができる」とすればよいでしょう。本文では第3文の主語はThermal recyclingとなっていますが、要約文では前文の繰り返しになるので、this kind of recycling「この種のリサイクル」などと指示語を使って表現するのがよいでしょう。8点満点で、各区分4点として減点法で採点します。

[**要約例**] This kind of recycling can suppress the generation of global-warming inducing methane gas, which is produced when plastics degrade.

　「プラスチックが劣化した時に生み出される、地球温暖化を誘発するメタンガスの発生を、この種のリサイクルは抑えることができる」

[**注1**]「メタンガスの発生を抑える」は、reduce the production of methane gas でも可。

[**注2**] global warming「地球温暖化」は通例無冠詞で使用する。ここではハイフンを用いて複合語にしている。

[**注3**]「地球温暖化を誘発するメタンガス」を関係代名詞を用いて書くと methane gas, which induces [contributes to] global warming となる。induce ～は「～を誘発する」という意味。

準1級

08

[**注4**]「劣化する」はdegradeのほか、deteriorateやbreak downも可。

第3段落

Thermal recycling is not a perfect solution, however. When waste is burned at a waste incineration plant, exhaust gases containing dioxins and other toxic substances are emitted. While thermal recycling suppresses the emission of methane gas, it does emit carbon dioxide, which is also bad for the environment.

しかし、サーマルリサイクルは完全な解決策ではない。廃棄物を焼却場で燃やすと、ダイオキシンなどの有害物質を含む排ガスが発生する。サーマルリサイクルはメタンガスの排出を抑える反面、やはり環境に悪い二酸化炭素を排出するのである。

語彙リスト

☐ **16.**	waste incinerátion plant	名	廃棄物焼却施設
☐ **17.**	exháust gas	名	排ガス
☐ **18.**	dióxin	名	ダイオキシン
☐ **19.**	tóxic	形	有毒な

解説と要旨

第1文からこの段落でサーマルリサイクルの欠点が示されることがわかります。具体的な欠点をまとめて要約します。第2文は❶「サーマルリサイクルによってダイオキシンなどの有毒物質を排出する」とし、第3文は後半を中心にまとめ❷「サーマルリサイクルによって二酸化炭素が排出される」とすれば十分でしょう。8点満点で、各区分4点として減点法で採点します。

[**要約例**] On the downside, thermal recycling emits toxic substances such as dioxin and carbon dioxide.

「よくない面としては、サーマルリサイクルによってダイオキシンなどの有毒物質および二酸化炭素が発生するということだ」

[**注1**] on the downside「よくない面として」は覚えておきたい。

[**注2**] dioxinも有毒物質なので、dioxin and <u>other</u> toxic substancesもしくは、toxic substances such as [including] dioxinとなる。

STEP 2
モニター答案でポイントをつかむ

[モニター答案例1]［10 / 25点］

   There are some materials that could not be recycled in material or chemical recycling. In such a case, waste can be burned and the energy generated in this process can be recovered and utilized by thermal recycling. We can reduce the

✗ →suppress：−1点

amount of methane gas that promotes grobal warming more greatly than carbon

✗ →, which：−2点　　✗ →global：−1点

dioxide do. However, this process generates exhaust and toxic gases.　　(63 words)

✗ →does：−1点

[内容点] 第1段落の❶❷はOK。❸はヌケで−3点。第2段落は、❶は「プラスチックの劣化時に生まれるメタンガス」の部分がヌケで不十分。−2点。❷は文法的なミスはあるものの内容はOK。第3段落の❶は不十分で−1点。❷はヌケで−4点。以上、−10点。

[文法点] −5点。reduce は「今あるものを減らす」という意味なので、reduce the production of 〜とするか suppress を使う。methane gas は、どの methane gas であれ地球温暖化を促進するので、関係代名詞は非制限用法を用いる。

[総評] 関係代名詞の制限用法と非制限用法は、英作文の時には常に意識しておきたい。

[モニター答案例2]［9 / 25点］

   Thermal recycling is a recycling way that recovers and utilizes the energy that is created when materials that cannot be recycled in other ways are burned. This

✗ →could not：−2点

way can prevent methane gas that has a large influence on global warming from

▲ →badly affects：減点なし

generating when plastic deteriorates. However, when they are burned, they emit

✗ → being generated：−3点　　　　　　　✗ → it is：−1点　　✗ → it emits：−1点

gases that contains dioxins and toxic substances, and also they emit carbon dioxide.

✗ → toxic substances including dioxins：−2点　　✗ → it emits：−1点

(65 words)

［**内容点**］第1段落の❶はほぼ本文の丸写しなので不可で−3点。❷はOK。ただし仮定法を使うべき箇所である。文法で減点するものとする。❸はヌケで−3点。第2段落は、❶❷とも文法的なミスはあるものの内容はOK。第3段落も、文法的なミスはあるが内容はOKである。以上、−6点。

［**文法点**］−10点。influenceは主に「(人の考えや行動)に影響する」の意味で用いるので、本問のような物理的影響に使うのは避けたい。generateは「〜を発生させる」という意味の他動詞である。dioxinも「毒性物質」に含まれるので、本文ではdioxins and other toxic substancesと書かれている。同じ語句の反復を避けるためにtoxic substances such as [including] dioxinsとする。

［**総評**］generateのミスは看過できない。能動と受動のミスは初歩的なミスなので、準1級レベルのミスとは思えない。

模範解答

Aside from material recycling, there are several types of recycling methods used on waste materials, but one of these, thermal recycling, is particularly important in that it generates energy by burning materials that could not otherwise be recycled. One environmental advantage of thermal recycling is that it mitigates methane emissions from degrading plastic, though it does entail the emission of harmful gases such as carbon dioxide. (66 words)

準1級

マテリアルリサイクルのほか、廃棄物に対し使われるリサイクル方法にはいくつかの種類があるが、その中でもサーマルリサイクルは、他の方法ではリサイクルできない素材を燃焼させることでエネルギーを生み出すという点で特に重要である。サーマルリサイクルの環境面でのメリットの1つは、二酸化炭素などの有害ガスを実際排出するものの、プラスチックの分解に伴うメタンの排出が抑えられることである。

語彙リスト

☐ **1.**	mítigate ~	動	~を軽減する
☐ **2.**	entáil ~	動	(必然的に) ~を伴う

08

解 答 例

Animal cafes have been increasing in number over the last few years, due to both the benefit of contact with animals to people's mental health, and opportunities to find foster homes for animals. However, animals in such cafes sometimes become ill from the stress of prolonged contact with strangers in enclosed spaces. Moreover, some cafes use smuggled animals. Therefore, exotic pet cafes are illegal in some countries.

(67 words)

　動物とのふれあいが精神的な健康に役立つことや、動物の里親探しのきっかけになることもあって、ここ数年、動物カフェが増えている。しかし、密閉された空間で見知らぬ者と長時間接することで、動物たちがストレスを感じ、体調を崩すことがある。また、中には密輸された動物を使うカフェもある。そのため、エキゾチック・ペットカフェは国によっては違法となっている。

STEP **1**
問題文の要点をつかむ

第1段落

Rather than having a pet, some people like to go to animal cafes. In fact, the number of such cafes has been increasing in recent years because they allow people who cannot have pets for some reasons to have close contact with animals.

ペットを飼うよりも、動物カフェに通いたいという人がいる。事実、何らかの理由でペットを飼えない人でも動物と身近にふれあえるということで、こうしたカフェの数は近年増えている。

語彙リスト

☐ **1.** for some réason 　　　　　　 熟 何らかの理由で

☐ **2.** have close cóntact with ～ 　熟 ～と身近にふれあう

解説と要旨

　この段落の骨子は❶「ペットを飼えない人でも、動物カフェでは動物と身近にふれあえる」と❷「最近動物カフェが増えている」です。ただし❶は、制限語数の関係上、第2段落の「動物とふれあうことは精神の健康によい」と内容的に重複する部分が多いので、ここでは割愛します。第1段落では❷を要約文として書けば十分でしょう。8点満点で、各区分4点として減点法で採点します。

[**要約例**] Animal cafes have been increasing in number over the last few years.
　「ここ数年、動物カフェが増えている」

[**注1**] Animal cafes have been becoming popular over the past few years. でも可。

[**注2**] 本文のin recent years「ここ数年」をover the last few yearsで置き換えている。recentlyは「ここ数ヶ月」の意味で使うことが多いので避けたい。

第2段落

These dog and cat cafes are popular for good reason —— playing with animals has been proven to enhance the mental and emotional health of people. Another benefit of these cafes is that they facilitate pet adoptions. By visiting these cafes, people are more likely to bond with the animals, increasing the likelihood of finding a home for them.

　こうした犬カフェや猫カフェが人気なのには正当な理由がある——動物と戯れることで、人の精神的、情緒的な健康が増進されることが証明されているのだ。このようなカフェの別の利点は、動物の里親探しが容易になることだ。こうしたカフェを訪れることで、動物たちとの絆が深まるようになり、それらの里親が見つかる可能性が高まるのだ。

語彙リスト

☐ **3.**	be próved to (V)	熟	～だと証明されている
☐ **4.**	enhánce ～	動	～を高める
☐ **5.**	facílitate ～	動	～を容易にする
☐ **6.**	pet adóption	名	動物の里親になること

解説と要旨

　この段落ではアニマルカフェが人気を博している理由が書かれているので、❶「動物とふれあうことは精神の健康によい」、❷「カフェの犬や猫の里親が見つけやすくなる」という2つの理由を要約文に含めればよいでしょう。解答例では第1段落の要約文に、第2段落の内容をdue to ～で始まる理由を表す句で表現し、つなげています。8点満点で、各区分4点として減点法で採点します。

[要約例] due to both the benefit of contact with animals to people's mental health, and opportunities to find foster homes for animals.

　「動物とのふれあいが人の精神的な健康に役立つことや、動物の里親探しのきっかけになることもあって」

[注1] 「精神の健康に役立つ」は、文にしてcontact with animals makes you feel relaxedなどと書くこともできる。

[注2] foster homeは「里子を預かる家庭」という意味。「里親が見つけやすくなる」は、create an opportunity for you to adopt animals や、create an opportunity for animals to be given new houses でも可。

On the downside, long contact with strangers in the closed space of a cafe can put stress on the animals, which makes them more susceptible to disease. Furthermore, there are some animal cafes that use rare animals, such as owls and hedgehogs, obtained by smuggling. In fact, for the benefit of the health of the animals, this type of exotic pet cafe is illegal in Europe, the U.S., and Taiwan.

デメリットとしては、カフェという閉ざされた空間で見知らぬ者と長く接することは、動物たちにストレスを与え、病気にかかりやすくする可能性がある。さらに密輸によって入手したフクロウやハリネズミなどの希少動物を使う動物カフェもある。実際、動物たちの健康のため、欧米や台湾ではこの種のエキゾチック・ペットカフェは違法とされている。

語彙リスト

☐ **7.**	put stress on ～	熟	～にストレスを与える
☐ **8.**	be suscéptible to ～	熟	(病気など) にかかりやすい
☐ **9.**	hédgehog	名	ハリネズミ
☐ **10.**	smúggling	名	密輸
☐ **11.**	illégal	形	非合法の

解説と要旨

　第1文は❶「そうしたカフェの動物は閉鎖空間での長時間の人間との接触によりストレスがかかり、病気になりやすい」とする。第2文は❷「中には密輸された動物を扱うカフェがある」とする。第3文は❸「そのためエキゾチック・ペットカフェは違法とされている国もある」とする。9点満点で、各区分3点として減点法で採点します。

[**要約例**] Animals in such cafes sometimes become ill from the stress of prolonged contact with strangers in enclosed spaces. Moreover, some cafes use smuggled animals. Therefore, exotic pet cafes are illegal in some countries.

　「密閉された空間で見知らぬ者と長時間接することで、動物たちがストレスを感じ、体調を崩すことがある。また、中には密輸された動物を使うカフェもある。そのため、エキゾチック・ペットカフェは国によっては違法となっている」

[**注1**] prolonged contact は、本文通りに long contact でも可。

[**注2**] 「密閉された」は enclosed とする。

[**注3**] smuggle は「～を密輸する」という意味。smuggled animals は illegally captured animals「違法に捕獲された動物」でも可。

STEP 2
モニター答案でポイントをつかむ

[モニター答案例1] [24 / 25点]

The number of animal cafes has been increasing recently because those who do not have their own pets can have contact with animals. Those cafes enhance the mental and emotional health and facilitate pet adoptions. However, such cafes may have a negative impact on rare exotic animals. Long contact with strangers can put stress on the animals. Therefore, some cafes are banned in some countries.

✗ →such：−1点

(65 words)

[**内容点**] 第1段落は❶❷ともにOK。第2段落も❶❷ともにOK。第3段落は❶❷❸ともにOK。非常によくできた答案である。

[**文法点**] −1点。

[**総評**] 非常によく出来ている。英作文だけなら1級も狙える。

[モニター答案例2] [11 / 25点]

These days, animal cafes are becoming popular because they enable people to have close contact with animals without own pets. Thanks to these cafes, they will

✗ →owning：−2点

keep their mental and emotional health. Moreover, they may help the animals to find a new house. However, ✗ rare animals of these shops may go away. Also,

ヌケ→ smuggling of：−2点 ✗ →for：−1点 ✗ →トル：−2点

animals tend to feel stressed due to long and close contact with strangers.

(66 words)

［**内容点**］第1段落は❶❷ともにOK。第2段落も❶❷ともにOK。第3段落は❶は「病気になる」がないので−2点。❷は意味がずれているので、−2点。❸がヌケで−3点。以上、−7点。

［**文法点**］−7点。ownは、one's own ～の形で使うか、動詞として使う。動詞は「～を所有する」の意味になり、withoutという前置詞の後に置くならowningという動名詞にする。

［**総評**］内容・文法ともに第3段落が不十分である。最後まで気を抜かずに。

STEP 3
ネイティブスピーカーの解答に学ぶ

模範解答

Animal cafes are becoming increasingly popular because they give people the chance to interact with cats and dogs, which is known to have several health benefits and also encourage pet adoption. However, keeping animals in confined spaces may contribute to increased stress and disease. What's more, exotic animals housed in cafes are sometimes illegally traded; for this reason such cafes are banned in several countries.

(65 words)

　動物カフェの人気が高まっているのは、人々が犬や猫とふれあう機会を提供することで、そうしたことにいくつかの健康上の利点があることが知られており、また、動物の里親も見つかりやすくなるからだ。しかし、閉ざされた空間で動物を飼育することは、ストレスや病気の増加の一因となる可能性がある。さらに、カフェに収容されているエキゾチックな動物は違法に取引されることもある。この理由で、そうしたカフェはいくつかの国で禁止されている。

解 答 例

New Zealand introduced the Living Standards Framework in 2019 to evaluate its national progress, considering economic, social, environmental, and cultural factors. Proponents argue that it assists in policy-making, thereby enhancing people's quality of life because it matches public values. Critics argue that it should only be used as a reference for traditional economic indicators because it is too subjective to be reliable, and can distract the government from economic growth.

(70 words)

　ニュージーランドは2019年、経済的、社会的、環境的、文化的要因を考慮して、国の発展を評価する「生活水準フレームワーク」を導入した。推進派は、この指標は国民の価値観に合致しているので、政策立案を支援し、それによって人々の生活の質を高めると主張している。批判派は、この指標はあまりに主観的なので信頼できず、政府の目を経済成長からそらす可能性があるため、従来の経済指標の参考としてのみ使用されるべきであると主張している。

STEP 1
問題文の要点をつかむ

第1段落

Since 2019, New Zealand has been using a well-being indicator to measure its national development. The indicator, called the Living Standards Framework, measures not only economic factors but also social, environmental, and cultural aspects of well-being. However, some people think that the well-being indicator is too vague and subjective.

2019年以来、ニュージーランドは国の発展を測定するために幸福度指標を使用している。生活水準フレームワークと呼ばれるこの指標は、経済的要因だけでなく、幸福の社会的、環境的、文化的な側面も測定の対象としている。しかし、幸福度指標はあまりにも曖昧で主観的であると考える人もいる。

語彙リスト

□ **1.**	wéll-béing	名	幸福
□ **2.**	índicàtor	名	指標
□ **3.**	méasure 〜	動	〜を測定する
□ **4.**	áspect	名	面
□ **5.**	vague	形	曖昧な
□ **6.**	subjéctive	形	主観的な

解説と要旨

　第1文の要旨は、❶「2019年以来、ニュージーランドは、国の発展を測定するために（生活水準フレームワークと呼ばれる）幸福度指標を使用している」、第2文は❷「その測定には経済的要因だけでなく、幸福の社会的、環境的、文化的な側面も考慮している」です。本文に書かれているほぼすべての要素を必要とするので、どう言い換えるかがポイントとなりそうです。across several key areas「いくつかの鍵となる領域を

またぎ」などと簡潔に書くこともできます。第3文は「この指標は曖昧で主観的であると言って批判する人がいる」ですが、この具体化が後半で出てくるので、第1段落の要約には入れないことにします。8点満点で、各区分4点として、減点法で採点します。

[**要約例**] New Zealand introduced the Living Standards Framework in 2019 to evaluate its national progress, considering economic, social, environmental, and cultural factors.

「ニュージーランドは2019年、経済的、社会的、環境的、文化的要因を考慮して、国の発展を評価する『生活水準フレームワーク』を導入した」

[**注1**] the Living Standards Framework という固有名詞を使わずに、a well-being indicator とすることもできる。

[**注2**]「国の発展を測定する」は、本文の measure its (national) development を引用して、measure its development socially, environmentally and culturally, as well as its economic growth とすることもできる。

[**注3**]「～を考慮して」は、taking into account [consideration] ～でも可。

第2段落

Supporters of the well-being indicator say that it reflects the true values and priorities of the people. They argue that the well-being indicator can help the government make better policies that improve the quality of life for everyone. For example, the well-being indicator can guide the government to invest more in health, education, and environmental protection.

幸福度指標の支持者たちは、それが国民の真の価値観と優先事項を反映していると述べている。彼らは、幸福度指標が、誰にとっても生活の質を向上させる、よりよい政策を政府がつくるのに役立つと主張している。たとえば、幸福度指標は、政府が健康、教育、環境保護にさらに投資するように導くことができる。

語彙リスト

☐ **7.**	refléct ～	動	～を反映している
☐ **8.**	priórity	名	優先事項
☐ **9.**	invést in ～	熟	～に投資する

第1文は❶「この指標の支持者は、これが人々の価値観や優先事項に合致していると述べている」とします。「優先事項」は「価値観」に含まれると考えられるので、「優先事項」はなくても可とします。またwhat people value most「人々が最も重要と思っているもの」とすることもできます。第2文、第3文は❷「政府の政策立案を支援し、それによる人々の生活の質の引き上げに役立つと主張している」です。後半の「それによる人々の生活の質の引き上げに役立つ」は、なくても減点しないことにします。また、第3文は第2文の「生活の質」の具体例ですが、語数制限を考えると省くしかないでしょう。なお、❷が主張であり、その理由が❶であることに注意してください。8点満点で、各区分4点として、減点法で採点します。

[要約例] Proponents argue that it assists in policy-making, thereby enhancing people's quality of life because it matches public values.
「推進派は、この指標は国民の価値観に合致しているので政策立案を支援し、それによって人々の生活の質を高めると主張している」
[注1] proponent「支持者」は、advocate でも可。
[注2] matches public values は is in line with public values でも可。また説明的に、shows what people value most とすることもできる。
[注3] enhance は、簡単な語を用いるなら raise や improve となる。

第3段落

Although the well-being indicator has some supporters, critics have pointed out problems with it. They say that the well-being indicator is not reliable or consistent, as it depends on people's subjective feelings and opinions. Additionally, they claim that the well-being indicator can distract the government from focusing on economic growth and stability, which are essential for the country's development. They suggest that the well-being indicator should be used as a supplement, not a substitute, for traditional economic indicators.

幸福度指標には支持者もいるが、批判的な人たちは問題点をいくつか指摘している。彼らによると、幸福度指標は人々の主観的な感情や意見に左右されるため、信頼性や一貫性に欠けるということだ。さらに、幸福度指標は、国の発展に不可欠な経済成長と安定に焦点を当てることから政府の目をそらす可能性があると主張している。彼らは、幸福度指標は従来の経済指標の代替ではなく、補完として使われるべきであると提案している。

準1級

10

☐ **10.**	relíable	形	信頼できる	
☐ **11.**	consístent	形	一貫した	
☐ **12.**	distráct A from B	熟	Aの注意をBからそらす	
☐ **13.**	stabílity	名	安定性	
☐ **14.**	súpplement for ~	熟	~を補完するもの	
☐ **15.**	súbstitùte for ~	熟	~の代替物	

解説と要旨

　この段落では批判側の意見が述べられています。第1文と第2文の要旨は ❶「幸福度指標は、人々の感情や意見に左右され、一貫性に欠けるので信頼できない」ということです。「人々の感情や意見に左右される」は、subjective「主観的である」でまとめれば、語数を減らすことができます。「信頼できない」と「一貫性がない」は、どちらか1つでよいでしょう。第3文は ❷「幸福度指標は、政府の目を経済成長からそらしてしまう」が要旨です。第4文の要旨は ❸「幸福度指標は、従来の経済指標の参照にとどめるべきだ」です。9点満点で、各区分3点として、減点法で採点します。

[**要約例**] Critics argue that it should only be used as a reference for traditional economic indicators because it is too subjective to be reliable, and can distract the government from economic growth.

「批判派は、この指標はあまりに主観的なので信頼できず、政府の目を経済成長からそらす可能性があるため、従来の経済指標の参考としてのみ使用されるべきであると主張している」

[**注1**] critics は opponents「反対派」も可。

[**注2**] ❸ は、it should be part of an indicator, not a replacement for the traditional one と書くこともできる。なお、解答例の a reference for ~は本文の a supplement for ~の言い換え。

[**注3**] be subjective は、語数が許すなら be influenced by popular [public] sentiment(s)「国民感情を左右される」としてもよい。

[**注4**] distract the government from ~ は、divert the government's attention from ~や prevent the government from concentrating on economic growth とすることもできる。

STEP 2
モニター答案でポイントをつかむ

[モニター答案例1]［14 / 25点］

　　There are two different sides about New Zealand's well-being indicator. One
　　　　　　　✗ →opinions concerning：－2点
says that it is useful to know what people really think is important, and it allows

the government to make better decisions about the usage of its budget. However,
　　　　　　　　　　　　　　　　　　✗ →use：－2点
the other side argues that the government should not completely rely on the

indicator, because it is too subjective. They think that traditional indicators should

not be replaced by it.　　　　　　　　　　　　　　　　　　　　　　(70 words)

［**内容点**］第1段落は、❶の「2019年以来」が抜けているが減点しないものとする。❷
はヌケで、－4点。第2段落の❶はOK。❷は「人々の生活を改善」が抜けているが減
点しない。第3段落は、❶はOK。❷のヌケで－3点。❸はOK。以上、－7点。
［**文法点**］－4点。
［**総評**］荒削りであるがよい答案である。点数はそれほど高くないが、実力は高い。

[モニター答案例2]［7 / 25点］

　　There are two opinions for a well-being indicator which New Zealand has
　　　　　　　　　　✗ →concerning the：－2点
been using since 2019 to measure its development. One side says that it can help

the government make ✗ better society that everyone can live good quality of life.
　　　　　　　　　　ヌケ→a：－1点　✗ →in which：－2点　✗ →has：－2点
The other side says that it is too subjective to rely on, and it should be used

supplementarily because it distracts country's development.　　　(63 words)
　　　　✗ →the government from economic development which is essential to its growth：－3点

［**内容点**］第1段落の❶はOKだが、❷のヌケで−4点。第2段落は❶のヌケで−4点。❷は文法的ミスがあるものの内容はOK。第3段落は、❶はOK。❷は不十分だが、文法点での減点とする。❸はOK。以上、−8点

［**文法点**］−10点。societyやenvironmentやsituationなどはthat節と同格関係にはならないので、in whichで接続する。live［lead］a good quality lifeとは言えるが、live［lead］good quality of lifeとは言えない。

［**総評**］全体像はつかんでいるが、各段落の情報を盛り込むことができていない。情報は「ギューギューに詰め込む」こと。

STEP3
ネイティブスピーカーの解答に学ぶ

模範解答

New Zealand has for several years used an economic instrument known as the Living Standards Framework, which rates citizen well-being across several key areas. Advocates of this system contend that it can inform a range of policy related to public welfare. However, its detractors point to the inherent subjectivity and inconsistency of the rating system as a major flaw, and suggest limiting its application to an advisory role.

(68 words)

ニュージーランドでは、数年前から生活水準フレームワークと呼ばれる経済指標が用いられている。それは、市民の幸福をいくつかの鍵となる領域をまたぎ測定するものである。このシステムを支持する人々は、このシステムが公共の福祉に関連するさまざまな政策の情報源になると主張している。しかし、このシステムを批判する人たちは、この評価システムに内在する主観性と一貫性のなさが大きな欠点であるとし、その適用を諮問的な役割に限定することを提案している。

語彙リスト

☐ **1.**	ádvocate	图	支持者
☐ **2.**	conténd that SV	熟	SVと主張する
☐ **3.**	infórm 〜	動	〜に情報を与える

☐ **4.**	detráctor	名	中傷する人
☐ **5.**	point to A as B	熟	AをBであると指摘する
☐ **6.**	inhérent	形	内在する
☐ **7.**	flaw	名	欠陥
☐ **8.**	advísory	形	諮問的な、助言の

解 答 例

Since the mid-20th century, Bahrain and other Gulf countries have been constructing large artificial islands for land expansion and the creation of luxury resort areas. Experts are concerned about the environmental impact of the projects, because these islands are being built on coral reefs. These are habitats for many organisms and act as natural water filters, so their depletion has lowered the quality of the water. Bahrain has lost a large area of both reef and mangrove forest. If reclamation continues at this pace, the local environment will change dramatically within the next decade. However, Bahrain has ordered a ban on sand extraction in order to restore the seabed.

(109 words)

　20世紀半ば以降、バーレーンをはじめとする湾岸諸国は、国土の拡張と高級リゾート地の造成を目的に、大規模な人工島の建設を進めてきた。専門家はこうしたプロジェクトが環境に及ぼす影響を懸念している。なぜなら、これらの人工島はサンゴ礁の上に建設されているからだ。サンゴ礁は多くの生物にとっての生息地であり、天然の水のフィルターとして機能している。だから、それらの減少によって水質が低下したのだ。バーレーンはサンゴ礁とマングローブ林の両方のかなりの面積を失った。このままの割合で埋め立てが進めば、地域の環境は今後10年以内に劇的に変化するだろう。しかし、バーレーンは海底を回復させるため、砂の採取の禁止を命じた。

STEP 1
問題文の要点をつかむ

第1段落

Sea reclamation projects in Bahrain, where the seabed is used to build new islands, have been carried out mainly along the coastline since the 1960s, expanding the country from 690 square km to over 780 square km by 2021 — making Bahrain today slightly larger in area than Singapore. Neighboring Gulf states with even larger land areas have also been building large-scale artificial islands for decades. Some are especially striking, such as Palm Jumeirah in Dubai, which started being constructed in 1990. It is now a group of offshore islands that together resemble a palm tree and are home to luxury hotels.

バーレーンでは海底を用いた新しい島の建設が進んでいるが、その海の埋め立て事業は1960年代から海岸線を中心に行われ、国土は2021年までに690平方キロメートルから780平方キロメートル以上に拡大した。その結果、現在のバーレーンの面積はシンガポールをわずかに上回ることになった。さらに広い国土を有する近隣の湾岸諸国も、数十年にわたって大規模な人工島を建設してきた。中には1990年に建設が始まったドバイのパーム・ジュメイラのように、特に目を引くものもある。それは、現在、離島群全体でヤシの木に似た形になっており、高級ホテルが建ち並んでいる。

語彙リスト

- □ **1.** rèclamátion 〔名〕（埋め立て、干拓、灌漑などによる）土地改良
- □ **2.** Gúlf stàtes 〔名〕湾岸諸国
  ※本文ではペルシャ湾岸諸国（イラン、イラク、クウェート、サウジアラビア、バーレーン、カタール、アラブ首長国連邦、オマーン）のことを指す。
- □ **3.** be home to ～ 〔熟〕～の拠点である、［生息地］である

　バーレーンとドバイの例および第2文の記述から、**❶**「20世紀半ばから、過去数十年にわたり」、「(バーレーンなどの) 中東のペルシャ湾岸諸国」が必要でしょう。第1文のバーレーンの例は**❷**「国土拡大のための大規模な人工島建設」とします。具体的には「バーレーンは、人工島によって国土面積が100キロ平方キロメートルも拡大してシンガポールの面積を上回ることになった」となりますが、これを入れるほど語数に余裕はないでしょう。さらに第3〜4文のドバイの例は**❸**「大規模リゾート地を作るための(大規模な人工島建設)」でよいでしょう。「海の埋め立てによって」through [by means of] sea reclamation も触れたいところですが、語数を抑えたい場合は artificial islands でも十分です。9点満点で、各区分3点として減点法で採点します。

[要約例] Since the mid-20 century, Bahrain and other Gulf countries have been constructing large artificial islands for land expansion and the creation of luxury resort areas.

　「20世紀半ば以降、バーレーンをはじめとする湾岸諸国は、国土の拡張と高級リゾート地の造成を目的に、大規模な人工島の建設を進めてきた」

第2段落

　Meanwhile, experts studying the history of artificial island construction are concerned about the impact of projects to reclaim the sea and build islands. This is because these artificial islands are often built on coral reefs that are home to hundreds of tropical species. These reefs act as natural filters for the water, but the construction of artificial islands has reduced the area of this natural filter and has worsened the quality of the water in the Persian Gulf.

　一方、人工島建設の歴史を研究する専門家たちは、海を埋め立てて島を建設する事業の影響を懸念している。というのも、こうした人工島は、何百種類もの熱帯生物が生息するサンゴ礁の上に建設されることが多いからだ。これらのサンゴ礁は水をろ過する天然のフィルターとして機能しているが、人工島の建設によってこの天然のフィルターの面積が減少し、ペルシャ湾の水質が悪化している。

語彙リスト

☐ **4.**	recláim 〜	動	(沼地、海など) を干拓する、埋め立てる
☐ **5.**	córal rèef	名	サンゴ礁

　第1文は❶「専門家はこうしたプロジェクトが環境に及ぼす影響を懸念している」と
します。「専門家は…懸念している」はなくても、「環境を脅かしている」「環境に被害
を与えている」という内容でもOKです。第2文は❷「これらの島々はサンゴ礁の上に
作られており、サンゴ礁には多くの生物が生息している」とします。第3文は❸「（こ
れらのサンゴ礁は）水をろ過する天然のフィルターとして機能している」および❹「サン
ゴ礁の喪失により（ペルシャ湾の）水質が悪化している」とします。natural filters for
the water は、natural water filters とすれば語数を減らせます。8点満点で、各区分
2点として減点法で採点します。

[要約例] Experts are concerned about the environmental impact of the projects,
because these islands are being built on coral reefs. These are habitats for
many organisms and act as natural water filters, so their depletion has lowered
the quality of the water.

　「専門家はこうしたプロジェクトが環境に及ぼす影響を懸念している。なぜなら、こ
れらの島々はサンゴ礁の上に建設されているからだ。サンゴ礁は多くの生物にとって
の生息地であり、天然の水のフィルターとして機能している。だから、それらの減少
によって水質が低下したのだ」

第3段落

　In Bahrain, 182,000 square meters of coral reefs have been lost as a result of
frequent dredging of the sands of the seabed near Muharraq Island. Furthermore,
95% of the mangroves in Tubli Bay, which is located in the northeastern area of
Bahrain Island, were also found to have been lost due to dredging in land
reclamation projects. If the construction of these artificial islands continues,
within the next decade, all of the shallow coastal areas will become land, and the
offshore areas will become shallower, changing the environment of the Persian
Gulf. However, in 2019, an order to ban the extracting and dredging of sand, in a
bid to allow the kingdom's seabed to recover from decades of damage, was
announced by Bahraini Prime Minister Prince Khalifa bin Salman Al Khalifa.

　バーレーンでは、ムハラク島付近の海底の砂を頻繁に浚渫した結果、18万2,000平方メートル
のサンゴ礁が失われた。さらに、バーレーン島北東部に位置するトゥブリ湾のマングローブも、埋め
立て事業による浚渫で95%が失われていることが判明した。こうした人工島の建設が進めば、今

後10年以内に沿岸の浅瀬はすべて陸地となり、沖合の海は浅くなり、ペルシャ湾の環境は一変する。しかし2019年、王国の海底が数十年にわたるダメージから回復することを目指し、砂の採取と浚渫を禁止する命令がバーレーン首相のハリファ・ビン・サルマン・アル・ハリファ皇太子により発せられた。

解説と要旨

　第1〜2文は❶「バーレーンはサンゴ礁とマングローブ林の両方のかなりの面積を失った」とします。第3文は、❷「埋め立てがこのペースで進めば今後10年以内にペルシャ湾の環境は大きく変化するだろう」でよいでしょう。第4文は❸「バーレーンは海底の回復を目指して」、❹「砂の採取と浚渫を禁止した」とします。「浚渫」はなくてもよいでしょう。本文では2019年とあるので過去時制になっていますが、語数を削減するため解答では現在完了を用いています。8点満点で、各区分2点として減点法で採点します。

[**要約例**] Bahrain has lost a large area of both reef and mangrove forest. If reclamation continues at this pace, the local environment will change dramatically within the next decade. However, Bahrain has ordered a ban on sand extraction in order to restore the seabed.

　「バーレーンはサンゴ礁とマングローブ林の両方のかなりの面積を失った。このままの割合で埋め立てが進めば、地域の環境は今後10年以内に劇的に変化するだろう。しかし、バーレーンは海底を回復させるため、砂の採取の禁止を命じた」

STEP**2**
モ ニ タ ー 答 案 で ポ イ ン ト を つ か む

[**モニター答案例1**]［**14 / 25点**]

In Bahrain, sea reclamation projects have been carried out since ✕1960s, and

ヌケ→the：－1点

have expanded the country. Some of ✕artificial islands which were created in

ヌケ→the：－1点

such projects are home to luxury hotels now. However, as these artificial islands

are often built on coral reefs that are home to hundreds of tropical species and are

natural filters for the water, it is said that constructing artificial islands will worsen

✕ →トル：－1点

the environment of the ocean. The construction will change all of the shallow

coastal areas into land within the next decades. However, in 2019, ✕Bahraini

ヌケ→the：－1点

Prime Minister announced to ban the extracting and dredging sand, which affect the

✕ →a ban on：－2点

environment badly. (107 words)

[**内容点**] 第1段落❶は「湾岸諸国」のヌケで－2点、❷❸はOK。第2段落は❶❷❸
❹すべてOK。第3段落は❶がヌケで－2点。❷はOK。❸は「海底の回復を目指して」
がヌケで－1点。❹はOK。以上、－5点減点。
[**文法点**] －6点。
[**総評**] 概ねできているが、いやしくも1級を受験しようとする人が the 1960s の the
を抜かしているようではいけない。「文法は合っていて当たりまえ」が1級レベルであ
ることを心得よう。

01

[**モニター答案例2**]［**8 / 25点**]

In Bahrain and ✕Gulf States, sea reclamation projects are conducted. The

ヌケ→other：－1点

target of these projects is to build large-scale artificial islands. However, these

projects involve a risk of destroying the environment because coral reefs, which

are helpful to improve ✕ quality of the water and home to tropical species, are

ヌケ→ the：−1 点

used to build lands. Because of these projects, the majority of coral reefs have been

✕ → coral reefs and the majority of mangroves：−2 点

lost. If these projects continued and sands that are home to coral reefs were lost,

the environment would be completely changed. However, in 2019, a rule to ban

removing sand was announced. (96 words)

［**内容点**］第1段落の❶は「過去数十年にわたり」がヌケで−2点。❷は「国土拡大」がヌケで−1点。❸はヌケで−3点。第2段落の❶はOK。❷はサンゴ礁に関する記述が不十分なので−1点。❸はOK。❹がヌケで−2点。第3段落の❶はマングローブの記述が不十分なので−1点。❷は「今後10年以内に」のヌケで−1点、❸はヌケで−2点。❹はOK。以上、−13点。

［**文法点**］−4点。

［**総評**］きちんとした本文の分析もなく、「何となくこんなことが書いてあるよね」というフィーリングで書かれた答案である。これでは高得点は望めない。

STEP 3
ネイティブスピーカーの解答に学ぶ

模範解答

Over the past 60 years, several Persian Gulf states such as Bahrain have expanded in area thanks to a series of sea reclamation and island-building projects. The islands created are visually striking and home to luxury developments. However, the biodiverse coral reefs these islands are built on have been threatened, and their natural filtration function has been lessened, leading to a drop in Gulf seawater quality. In particular, Bahrain has lost a significant area of both reef and mangrove forest. If the reclamation continues at this rate, the local environment will be radically altered, so laws have been passed to protect and restore it. (104 words)

過去60年にわたって、バーレーンなどのペルシャ湾岸諸国は、一連の海面埋め立てと島建設プロジェクトによって面積を拡大してきた。造成された島々は見た目も美しく、豪華な造成地となっている。しかし、これらの島々がその上に築かれた生物多様性の高いサンゴ礁は脅かされ、天然のろ過機能が低下し、湾内の海水の水質低下を招いている。特にバーレーンでは、サンゴ礁とマングローブ林の両方がかなりの面積で失われている。このまま埋め立てが進めば、地域の環境は激変してしまうため、そうした環境の保護と回復のための法律が制定された。

語彙リスト

□ **1.**	bìodivérse	形 生物多様性のある

1級
01

解 答 例

Palm oil, which is the most widely used oil in food processing, is predominantly produced in Indonesia, Malaysia and Thailand. Production is highest in Sumatra, which has lost over half of its forests to palm oil production in the last 30 years. This threatens wildlife, especially orangutans, who have been displaced, face starvation and poaching, and are now a critically endangered species. Palm oil has 6 to 10 times more yield than other oils, making it almost impossible to replace. For the sake of reforestation, its production, distribution, and sale are now regulated by a sustainable palm oil certification system, and consumers can protect the environment by choosing certified products.

(109 words)

　主に食品加工で最も広く使われている油であるパーム油は、そのほとんどがインドネシア、マレーシア、タイで生産されている。生産量が最も多いのはスマトラ島で、過去30年間にパーム油生産のために森林の半分以上が失われた。これによって野生動物、特にオランウータンは脅かされており、居場所を奪われ、飢餓や密猟に直面し、今では絶滅の危機にある種である。パーム油は他の油に比べて生産性が6～10倍高いため、他のものに取り代えることはほぼ不可能だ。現在、森林再生のために、パーム油の生産、流通、販売は持続可能なパーム油認証制度によって規制されており、消費者は認証製品を選ぶことで環境を守ることができる。

STEP 1
問題文の要点をつかむ

第1段落

Currently, about 70 million tons of palm oil are produced annually worldwide. Three countries, namely Indonesia, Malaysia, and Thailand, are responsible for about 90% of this production. Palm oil is the most widely used vegetable oil in the world. Although its use in food products, mainly in processed foods such as bread and potato chips, accounts for 80% of its total use, palm oil is also used in detergents and is the main ingredient in soap. Over the past 10 years, in Indonesia, palm oil production has doubled and continues to increase. In particular, production of palm oil is the highest in the world on Indonesia's Sumatra Island.

現在、世界中で年間約7,000万トンのパーム油が生産されている。インドネシア、マレーシア、タイの3カ国で、この生産量の約90%を占めている。パーム油は世界で最も広く使用されている植物油である。主にパンやポテトチップスなどの加工食品を中心とした食品への利用が全体の80%を占めるが、パーム油は洗剤にも使われ、石鹸の主原料でもある。インドネシアでは過去10年間で、パーム油の生産量が倍増し、現在も増え続けている。特に、インドネシアのスマトラ島でのパーム油生産量は世界一である。

語彙リスト

□ **1.**	ánnually	副	毎年、1年間に
□ **2.**	námely	副	すなわち
□ **3.**	prócessed fòod	名	加工食品
□ **4.**	accóunt for 〜	熟	(割合など) を占める
□ **5.**	detérgent	名	洗剤
□ **6.**	ingrédient	名	原料

1級

02

第1～3文は、❶「パーム油は、世界で最も普及している油である」、❷「インドネシア、マレーシア、タイを主産地とする」とします。第4文は❸「主に食品加工に使われている」とすれば十分です。第5～6文の「（インドネシアの）スマトラ島でのパーム油生産量は世界一である」というポイントは、解答では、次の段落の要旨に加えることにします。8点満点で、各区分3点として減点法で採点します。0点になった場合、それ以上減点はしません。

[**要 約 例**] Palm oil, which is the most widely used oil in food processing, is predominantly produced in Indonesia, Malaysia and Thailand.

「主に食品加工で最も広く使われている油であるパーム油は、そのほとんどがインドネシア、マレーシア、タイで生産されている」

第2段落

However, compared to 30 years ago, the island's forests have been reduced to less than half, and lowland forests are almost gone. They have been cleared on a large scale to cultivate oil palms and have been transformed into oil palm plantations. Their exponential expansion on Sumatra Island has led to widespread deforestation, or the destruction of rainforests, and the displacement of wildlife, particularly orangutans. The continued damage to where they live has unfavorable outcomes, as they not only lose their homes but also confront escalating risks of starvation and dangerous encounters with humans, who poach them for food or to sell as pets. At present, the Sumatran orangutan is considered critically endangered, with an estimated population of only 6,600 individuals.

しかし、30年前と比較すると、島の森林は半分以下に減少し、低地の森林はほとんどなくなっている。アブラヤシ栽培のために大規模な伐採が行われ、アブラヤシのプランテーションへと姿を変えてしまったのだ。スマトラ島でのプランテーションの急激な拡大により、広域の森林伐採、つまり熱帯雨林の破壊が進み、野生動物、特にオランウータンの居場所が奪われている。彼らの生息地の損壊が続くことで、オランウータンはすみかを失うだけでなく、飢餓や、食用やペット用に密猟する人間との危険な遭遇のリスクも高まっており、好ましくない状況になってきている。現在、スマトラオランウータンは絶滅の危機に瀕しており、その個体数はわずか6,600頭と推定されている。

□ **7.** lówland   形 低地の

☐ **8.**	clear ~	動	（場所などから）～を取り除く
☐ **9.**	on a lárge scàle	熟	大規模に
☐ **10.**	cúltivàte ~	動	～を栽培する
☐ **11.**	be transfórmed into ~	熟	～に変換される
☐ **12.**	èxponéntial	形	急激な（増加・減少）
☐ **13.**	defòrestátion	名	森林伐採
☐ **14.**	displácement	名	居場所を奪うこと
☐ **15.**	óutcòme	名	結果
☐ **16.**	poach ~	動	～を密猟する
☐ **17.**	crítically	副	危険なほど

解説と要旨

第1～2文は❶「生産量が最も多いスマトラではアブラヤシ栽培（＝パーム油生産）のため」❷「過去30年で森林伐採が急激に進んだ」という内容が書ければよいでしょう。「過去30年間で」はなくても減点しないものとします。第3～5文は❸「野生動物、特にオランウータンは、居場所を奪われ、飢餓や密猟に直面し、絶滅の危機に瀕している」という内容を書けばよいでしょう。語数を考えれば具体的な個体数までは必要ないでしょう。9点満点で、各区分3点として減点法で採点します。

[**要 約 例**] Production is highest in Sumatra, which has lost over half of its forests to palm oil production in the last 30 years. This threatens wildlife, especially orangutans, who have been displaced, face starvation and poaching, and are now a critically endangered species.

「生産量が最も多いのはスマトラ島で、過去30年間にパーム油生産のために森林の半分以上が失われた。これによって野生動物、特にオランウータンは脅かされており、居場所を奪われ、飢餓や密猟に直面し、今では絶滅の危機にある種である」

第3段落

In order to ensure deforestation-free production, further reforestation is necessary, especially considering the growing global population. While there are alternatives to using palm oil, its unparalleled yield — 6 to 10 times more than other oils — makes it a challenging switch. To address environmental concerns, a certification system for sustainable palm oil now strictly regulates its production, distribution, and sales. Consumers can contribute to environmental sustainability by choosing certified sustainable products.

　森林破壊をしない生産を確保するためには、特に世界人口の増加を考えると、さらなる森林再生が必要である。パーム油に代わる選択肢はあるものの、その比類なき生産性（他の油の6〜10倍）により、パーム油からの転換は困難である。環境への懸念に対処するため、現在では持続可能なパーム油の認証制度が、その生産、流通、販売を厳しく規制している。消費者は、認証された持続可能な製品を選ぶことで、環境の持続可能性に貢献することができる。

語彙リスト

☐ **18.**	defòrestátion-frèe	形	森林を破壊しない
☐ **19.**	rèforestátion	名	森林再生
☐ **20.**	altérnative to 〜	熟	〜に代わる方法
☐ **21.**	unpáralleled	形	比類なき
☐ **22.**	yield	名	生産高
☐ **23.**	chállenging	形	困難な
☐ **24.**	addréss 〜	動	〜に取り組む
☐ **25.**	cèrtificátion sỳstem	名	認証制度
☐ **26.**	régulàte	動	〜を規制する
☐ **27.**	dìstribútion	名	流通

解説と要旨

　第1文は「世界人口を考慮した森林再生の必要性」を述べています。ここは簡潔に❶「森林再生のために」ぐらいにとどめて、第3文の内容と組み合わせて表現すればよいでしょう。第2文は❷「パーム油は他の油に比べて生産性が6〜10倍高いため、その使用を止めることは難しい」という内容です。「6〜10倍」という数字はなくても「生産性がずっと高い」ということが書かれていればよいでしょう。第3文は❸「環境への懸念に対処するため、パーム油の生産、流通、販売は持続可能なパーム油認証制度によって規制されている」という内容です。最終文は❹「消費者は認証製品を選ぶことで環境に貢献することができる」となります。8点満点で、各区分2点として減点法で採点します。

[要約例] Palm oil has 6 to 10 times more yield than other oils, making it almost impossible to replace. For the sake of reforestation, its production, distribution, and sale are now regulated by a sustainable palm oil certification system, and consumers can protect the environment by choosing certified products.

「パーム油は他の油に比べて生産性が6〜10倍高いため、他のものに取り代えることはほぼ不可能だ。現在、森林再生のために、パーム油の生産、流通、販売は持続可能なパーム油認証制度によって規制されており、消費者は認証製品を選ぶことで環境を守ることができる」

STEP 2
モニター答案でポイントをつかむ

[モニター答案例1] [15 / 25点]

Palm oil is widely produced in the world every year. It is used not only in
→the most widely used oil：内容点で減点
processed foods but also in detergents. In Indonesia, whose production of palm oil

is the highest in the world, its production continues to increase, but cultivating a

large number of oil palms has led to an increase in deforestation and displacement

of wildlife. In particular, the Sumatran orangutan is thought to be endangered,

ensuring deforestation-free production requires further reforestation. Although no

other oil in the world is ✕ as productive as palm oil, consumers can contribute to
ヌケ→anywhere near：−2点
environmental sustainability by choosing certified sustainable products.

(99 words)

[**内容点**] 第1段落の❶は「最も」のヌケで−1点。❷はヌケで−3点。❸はOK。第2段落の❶❷はOK。❸は「居場所を奪われ飢餓や密猟に直面し」がヌケで−2点。第3段落の❶❷はOK。❸はヌケで−2点。❹はOK。以上、−8点減点。
[**文法点**] −2点。
[**総評**] 文法的なミスがなく、内容もだいたい網羅している。これぐらい書ければ合格

水準には達するだろう。

Currently, the amount of palm oil which is produced in the world is increasing. Palm oil are used in not only vegetable oil but also detergents. It is

✕ →is：－1点　　→not only in vegetable oil but also in detergents：－1点

mainly produced in Sumatra Island in Indonesia. However, more than fifty percent

of ✕forests were disappeared to plant palm trees compared with ✕it was thirty

ヌケ→ Sumatra's：－2点　✕ →have disappeared：－1点　✕ →due to palm tree cultivation：－3点　ヌケ→what：－3点

years ago. This deforestation causes some problems. For example, orangutans in the island lost their homes and they are more likely to encounter people who poach them for their own good. We can try to solve these problems by buying

✕ →トル：－2点

certified sustainable palm oil's products.　　　　　　　　　　　　　　(98 words)

✕ →oil：－1点

［**内容点**］第1段落の❶は「最も」のヌケで－1点。❷がヌケで－3点。❸はOK。第2段落の❶❷は文法的にミスが多いが内容はOKとする。❸は「飢餓に直面」「絶滅の危機に瀕している」のヌケで－2点。第3段落は❶❷はヌケで－4点。❸は不十分で－1点。❹はOK。以上、－11点。

［**文法点**］－14点。「前置詞＋名詞」と not only ～ but (also) ...や not ～ but ... を組み合わせる場合、「前置詞＋名詞」が一つのカタマリであるという認識が必要。to plant palm trees という箇所は、現状のままでは不可である。to 不定詞の主語は、主文の主語に一致するため、このような言い方は成立しない。

［**総評**］残念ながら文法力が低い。「きっちり書く」という習慣を身につけないと合格にはほど遠いだろう。

STEP 3
ネイティブスピーカーの解答に学ぶ

Worldwide, approximately 70 million tons of palm oil are produced annually, with Indonesia, Malaysia, and Thailand contributing 90% of this output. Palm oil is widely used in foods and household items such as detergents and soap. On Indonesia's Sumatra Island, palm oil production has doubled over the past decade, leading to extensive deforestation and threats to wildlife. In particular, with their habitat dwindling, orangutans increasingly face starvation and poaching. To mitigate this environmental damage, reforestation is vital. Although alternatives to palm oil exist, its superior yield makes it practically irreplaceable. Certification of sustainable palm oil aims to regulate production, distribution, and sale, and encourage consumers to choose environmentally friendly options.

(110 words)

世界中で年間約7,000万トンのパーム油が生産されており、インドネシア、マレーシア、タイがこの生産高の90％を占めている。パーム油は食品や洗剤、石鹸などの日用品に広く使用されている。インドネシアのスマトラ島では、パーム油の生産量が過去10年間で倍増し、大規模な森林破壊と野生生物への脅威につながっている。特に、オランウータンは、その生息地が減少しており、飢餓や密猟に直面することが多くなっている。こうした環境破壊を緩和するためには、森林再生が不可欠である。パーム油の代替品も存在するが、その優れた生産性により、パーム油は実質的に代替できないものとなっている。持続可能なパーム油の認証は、生産、流通、販売を規制し、消費者が環境に優しい選択肢を選ぶよう促すことを目的としている。

語彙リスト

☐ 1.	dwíndle	動	減少する
☐ 2.	póaching	名	密猟
☐ 3.	mítigàte ～	動	～を緩和する

1級

02

173

解 答 例

　"Sweatshops" date back to the early part of the Industrial Revolution, and the term refers to workplaces with poor health and safety conditions. They exist even today, generating huge amounts of money. There are currently strong labor and environmental laws, so such workplaces operate secretly. They employ illegal workers from poor countries and are sometimes linked to gangs or corrupt police. About 168 million children worldwide are exploited in sweatshops in various industries. Many international organizations and leaders demand that sweatshops improve their conditions or close down. However, some economists argue that governments should not interfere if the workers are adults because sweatshops are vital to the domestic economy.

(110 words)

　「スウェットショップ」の歴史は産業革命の初期にまでさかのぼり、この言葉は健康面や安全面で非常に劣悪な環境の職場を指す。それらは今日でさえ存在し、莫大なお金を生み出している。現在では強力な労働法と環境法があるため、このような職場は秘密裏に運営されている。そうした職場は貧しい国から不法労働者を雇い入れ、時にはギャングや腐敗した警察とつながっている。世界中で約1億6,800万人の子どもたちが、さまざまな業界のスウェットショップで搾取されている。多くの国際機関や指導者たちは、スウェットショップの環境改善や閉鎖を要求している。しかし、一部の経済学者の中には、労働者が成人であれば、スウェットショップは国内経済には不可欠なので、政府は干渉すべきではないと主張する人もある。

STEP 1
問題文の要点をつかむ

第1段落

When the Industrial Revolution began in the 1800s, companies felt little reason to maintain even basic hygiene, safety, or environmental standards. In such circumstances, it was not uncommon for workers to be maimed or killed. Children were also found in these workplaces, particularly in clothing factories. The worst of these businesses were nicknamed "sweatshops." By the mid-20th century, these workplace practices had seemingly ended. However, sweatshops had by no means disappeared. In 2024, the total value of the sweatshop sector was estimated to be US$1.5 trillion greater than ever before.

1800年代に産業革命が始まった時、会社は基本的な衛生、安全、環境基準さえ、それらを維持する理由をほとんど感じていなかった。そのような状況では、労働者が障害を負ったり死亡したりすることも珍しくなかった。このような職場、特に衣料品工場には子どもも見受けられた。こうした会社の中でも最悪のものは「スウェットショップ（労働搾取工場）」と呼ばれた。20世紀半ばまでに、こうした労働慣行は終結したかのように見えた。しかし、スウェットショップがなくなったわけでは決してなかった。2024年には、スウェットショップ部門の総額は以前より1兆5,000億米ドル増加したと推定された。

語彙リスト

□ **1.**	the Indústrial Revolùtion	图	産業革命
□ **2.**	hýgiene	图	衛生
□ **3.**	uncómmon	形	めったにない
□ **4.**	maim ～	動	～に障害を与える、～を傷つける
□ **5.**	swéatshòp	图	搾取工場、低賃金で長時間労働の工場
□ **6.**	práctice	图	慣行
□ **7.**	séemingly	副	～と思われる

□	8.	by nó mèans	熟 決して～ない
			※「何の手段もなく」が直訳。
□	9.	be éstimàted to (V)	熟 ～と推定されている
□	10.	tríllion	名 兆

解説と要旨

　第1～2文は❶「産業革命が始まった頃の労働環境は健康面や安全面で非常に劣悪だった」という内容です。「産業革命が始まった頃の」は「産業革命の時代には」「1800年代には」でも可とします。第3文は「労働者の中には子どももいた」という内容ですが、第2段落にも登場するので、ここでは触れなくてもよいでしょう。第4～7文の記述から、❷「このような、いわゆる『スウェットショップ』は今日でも存在し」、❸「莫大なお金を生み出している」ということを書きます。sweatshop は exploitation factory と言い換えることも可能ですが、この段落は「スウェットショップ」の説明でもあるので、ここではそのままの語を使う方が良いでしょう。9点満点で、各区分3点として減点法で採点します。

[要約例] "Sweatshops" date back to the early part of the Industrial Revolution, and the term refers to workplaces with poor health and safety conditions. They exist even today, generating huge amounts of money.

　「『スウェットショップ』の歴史は産業革命の初期にまでさかのぼり、この言葉は健康面や安全面で非常に劣悪な環境の職場を指す。それらは今日でさえ存在し、莫大なお金を生み出している」

第2段落

　The sweatshops of today resemble their historical counterparts, but with important differences. Those in economies with strong labor and environmental laws tend to be fairly clandestine. Sometimes they even operate in obscure, unmarked buildings. Moreover, they often rely on undocumented workers from underdeveloped countries. Such workers are often scared of the local government and so will not lodge complaints no matter how badly they are abused. In some cases, sweatshop owners have ties to criminal gangs or corrupt police, giving the owners another layer of protection. These businesses are not only active in manufacturing but also in online fraud, human trafficking, and black market operations. Worldwide, an estimated 168 million children work in sweatshops, often in virtual slavery.

今日のスウェットショップは、歴史上のスウェットショップと似ているが、いくつかの重要な違いがある。労働法や環境法が整備された国におけるスウェットショップは、かなり秘密裏に行われる傾向がある。時には、人目につかず、目立たない建物で操業していることさえある。さらに、発展途上国からの、就労許可証を有していない労働者に依存することが多い。そのような労働者は現地の政府を恐れているため、どんなにひどい虐待を受けても苦情を申し立てないことが多い。場合によっては、スウェットショップの所有者が犯罪組織や腐敗した警察とつながりを持っていて、その所有者はさらに別の方法で守られていることもある。こうしたビジネスは製造業だけでなく、オンライン詐欺、人身売買、闇市場操作でも行われている。世界では推定1億6,800万人の子どもたちがスウェットショップで働いており、その多くは事実上の奴隷状態にある。

解説 と 要旨

第1~3文は、❶「現在では、強力な労働法と環境法があり、そうしたスウェットショップは秘密裏に運営されている」という内容です。clandestine は、secretly や surreptitiously などに置き換えればよいでしょう。第4~5文は、「そうしたスウェットショップは、おそらく就労ビザを持たず、怖くて地元政府に不平を訴えられない、貧しい国から来た労働者を雇用している (employ workers from poor countries who probably do not have working visas and are too scared to complain to the local government)」という意味で

1級

03

すが、制限語数を考えれば❷「貧しい国からの不法労働者を雇用している」で十分でしょう。第6文は❸「そうしたスウェットショップはギャングや腐敗した警察とつながりがある」という内容です。第7文は、語数を考えると「様々な分野で」で十分でしょう。第8文は❹「世界中で約1億6,800万人の子どもたちが、ほとんど奴隷のようにスウェットショップで働いている」という意味ですが、「ほとんど奴隷のように働いている」を「搾取されている」とすれば語数を減らせます。8点満点で、各区分2点として減点法で採点します。

[要 約 例] There are currently strong labor and environmental laws, so such workplaces operate secretly. They employ illegal workers from poor countries and are sometimes linked to gangs or corrupt police. About 168 million children worldwide are exploited in sweatshops in various industries.

　「現在では強力な労働法と環境法があるため、このような職場は秘密裏に運営されている。そうした職場は貧しい国から不法労働者を雇い入れ、時にはギャングや腐敗した警察とつながっている。世界中で約1億6,800万人の子どもたちが、さまざまな業界のスウェットショップで搾取されている」

第3段落

　　There are numerous labor, UN, and human rights organizations cracking down on sweatshops. However, the term "sweatshop" itself is contested. Some economists argue that, as long as the workers are free adults, there is no need for the government to impose regulations. Particularly, in regions plagued with extreme poverty, any factory — even one operating well below Western standards — can provide valuable sources of local income. Nevertheless, many activists, union leaders and politicians continue to demand that sweatshops either improve their operating conditions or close down.

　スウェットショップを取り締まる労働団体、国連機関、人権団体は数多く存在する。しかし、「スウェットショップ」という言葉自体に異論が唱えられている。労働者が自由な大人である限り、政府が規制する必要はないと主張する経済学者もいる。特に極度の貧困に悩まされている地域では、どんな工場であっても―たとえ欧米の基準をはるかに下回る操業をしている工場であっても―地域の貴重な収入源を提供してくれる可能性もある。それにもかかわらず、多くの活動家、組合指導者、政治家は、スウェットショップに労働条件の改善か、閉鎖かを迫り続けている。

☐ **24.**	crack down on ～	熟	～を取り締まる
☐ **25.**	contést ～	動	～に異議を唱える
☐ **26.**	as long as SV	接	SVである限り
☐ **27.**	impóse ～	動	～を課す、押しつける
☐ **28.**	plagued with ～	熟	～で悩まされている
☐ **29.**	well belów ～	熟	～をはるかに下回って
☐ **30.**	únion lèader	名	組合指導者

解説と要旨

　第1文と最終文は1つにまとめて❶「多くの国際団体や指導者がスウェットショップに対し、労働条件の改善や閉鎖を要求している」とします。第2～4文は❷「労働者が成人であれば、スウェットショップは国内経済には不可欠なので、政府は干渉すべきではないと主張する経済学者もいる」という内容です。8点満点で、各区分4点として減点法で採点します。

[**要約例**] Many international organizations and leaders demand that sweatshops improve their conditions or close down. However, some economists argue that governments should not interfere if the workers are adults because sweatshops are vital to the domestic economy.

　「多くの国際機関や指導者たちは、スウェットショップの環境改善や閉鎖を要求している。しかし、一部の経済学者の中には、労働者が成人であれば、スウェットショップは国内経済には不可欠なので、政府は干渉すべきではないと主張する人もある」

STEP 2
モ ニ タ ー 答 案 で ポ イ ン ト を つ か む

[**モニター答案例1**][**11 / 25点**]

In the 1800s, it was not unusual for employees to be oppressed or killed ✕ .

　　　　　　　　　　　　　　　ヌケ→in factories：－2点

Although these workplace practices seem to disappear, even today, these

　　　　　✕ →have disappeared：－2点

workplaces called sweatshops remain. Sweatshops today are different from what
△ →still exist：減点なし
they used to be in that the former tend to be unknown because they often employ
✗ →they   ✗ →hidden：−2点
illegal workers who fear being punished and therefore will not complain. Many
organizations crack down on sweatshops, but some economists argue that
government does not have to impose penalties on them unless the workers are
slaves. Some people encourage sweatshops to improve their working conditions or
close although they can provide sources of income for poor workers.　　(107 words)
✗ →local income：減点なし

［**内容点**］第1段落の❶❷は可だが、❸がヌケで−3点。第2段落の❶は「現在は取り
締まる法律がある」ことがヌケで−1点。❷はOK。❸❹がヌケで−4点。第3段落の
❶はやや雑で、また「指導者」がないが減点しない。❷はOK。以上、−8点。

［**文法点**］−6点。

［**総評**］第3段落の内容を50語近い語数で書いてしまったため、第1〜2段落の内容に
漏れが生じた。全体のバランスを考えた語数の割り振りが重要。

［**モニター答案例2**］［**8 / 25点**］

　　Through the Industrial Revolution, companies became more selfish than ever,

so that many people worked in very poor conditions. These businesses are called

sweatshops, which still exist. These days they are working in unadmitted
✗ →unmarked：−2点
buildings and hire foreign workers who do not complain ✗their working
ヌケ→about：−2点
conditions. They sometimes ally with corrupt organizations. Many labor and

human rights organizations try to abolish sweatshops, partly because workers
✗ →because their wages are extremely low：−2点
working there are not paid the minimum wage. However, some economists contend

that they ✗should not be abolished, but many activists ✗say that they should
ヌケ→ are a valuable source of income and：−3点　✗ →though：−2点　　ヌケ→still：減点なし

improve their conditions or close. (95 words)

［**内容点**］第1段落の❶❷は可だが、❸がヌケで−3点。第2段落は❶はOKだが、❷は「不法の」がヌケで−1点。❸はOK。❹はヌケで−2点。第3段落は、❶❷とも不適切な表現を除けばOK。文法点で減点するものとする。以上、−6点。
［**文法点**］−11点。
［**総評**］admitやcomplainといった基本語の運用は2級レベル。そうしたミスは絶対にしないように、基本を徹底すること。

STEP 3
ネ イ テ ィ ブ ス ピ ー カ ー の 解 答 に 学 ぶ

模 範 解 答

　During the Industrial Revolution, businesses largely neglected hygiene, safety, and environmental standards, leading to hazardous working conditions in factories which became known as sweatshops. Although these practices ostensibly ceased by the mid-20th century, sweatshops exist today, with an estimated global value of US$1.5 trillion. Many sweatshops operate secretly, often exploiting poor undocumented workers who fear reprisal from authorities. Some are linked to criminal organizations or corrupt officials who engage in illegal activities, including the virtual enslavement of children. To counter this, some activists and politicians advocate for improved conditions or the closure of sweatshops. The term "sweatshop" remains contentious, with debates over government intervention versus economic necessity in impoverished regions. (110 words)

1 級

03

　産業革命の頃、企業は衛生、安全、環境基準をほとんど無視し、そのため、スウェットショップとして知られるようになった工場での危険な労働条件が生まれた。こうした慣行は20世紀半ばまで

に表向きには姿を消したが、今日もスウェットショップは存在し、その規模は世界で1兆5,000億米ドルにのぼると推定されている。多くのスウェットショップは秘密裏に運営されており、当局からの懲罰を恐れる貧しい不法労働者を搾取していることが多い。中には、犯罪組織や汚職官僚とつながり、子どもの事実上の奴隷化など違法行為に手を染めているところもある。これに対抗するため、一部の活動家や政治家は、スウェットショップの労働条件の改善や閉鎖を主張している。政府の介入と貧困地域における経済的必要性をめぐる議論もあり、「スウェットショップ」という言葉は依然として論争の的となっている。

語彙リスト

□ 1.	házardous	形	危険な
□ 2.	osténsibly	副	表面上は
□ 3.	reprísal	名	報復
□ 4.	conténtious	形	論争を引き起こす
□ 5.	impóverished	形	貧窮した

N O T E

解答例

Large numbers of children in Africa have no access to education due to a lack of schools and trained teachers. This results in child labor and hinders national and regional development, since economic progress requires a workforce with a basic level of education. Gender disparities also persist in African education, with limited early childhood education access for girls and a gender gap in school enrollment, influenced by African society's prioritizing the education of boys over that of girls. However, expanding educational opportunities for girls and women has great economic and family health benefits. Specifically, educated girls can boost the GDP, while educated women can ensure their family health.

(108 words)

アフリカでは多くの子どもたちは教育を受けられない。これは学校や訓練を受けた教師の不足が原因である。その結果、児童労働を生み出し、国と地域の発展を妨げている。なぜなら、経済発展には、基本的な教育を受けた労働力が必要だからだ。アフリカの教育においても男女格差は根強く、女子の教育よりも男子の教育を優遇するアフリカ社会の影響により、女子が初等教育を受ける機会は限られており、就学における男女格差がある。しかし、女子や女性の教育機会を拡大することは、経済面でも、家族の健康面でも大きなメリットがある。具体的には、教育を受けた女子はGDPを増大させ、教育を受けた女性は家族の健康を守ることができる。

STEP 1
問題文の要点をつかむ

第1段落

Millions of children in West and Central Africa still lack access to education. Instead of studying, these children are typically engaged in various forms of labor. For instance, in Tanzania, 22.3% of children aged 5 to 14 are engaged in economic activities, from agriculture to mining. This is not always because parents prefer their children to work, but often because there is a dearth of options open to them.

西アフリカと中央アフリカの何百万人もの子どもたちは、いまだに教育を受ける機会をもっていない。こうした子どもたちは勉強する代わりに、さまざまな形態の労働に従事しているのが一般的だ。例えばタンザニアでは、5歳から14歳までの子どもの22.3％が、農業から採鉱業までさまざまな経済活動に従事している。これは、必ずしも親が子どもに働くことを望むからではなく、子どもたちに開かれた選択肢が乏しいためであることが多い。

語彙リスト

☐ **1.**	týpically	副	普通、典型的には
☐ **2.**	míning	名	採鉱業
☐ **3.**	dearth	名	(人々が必要とするものの) 欠乏

解説と要旨

第1文は、❶「西アフリカと中央アフリカの何百万人もの子どもたちは」、❷「いまだに教育を受ける機会がない」という内容です。「教育を受ける機会がない」は本文の語を利用すればhave no access to educationですが、receive no education、face educational deprivationとすれば語数を減らせます。「西アフリカと中央アフリカ」は単に「アフリカ」、「何百万人の子どもたち」は「かなり多くの子どもたち」でも可とします。第2文および第4文は、第2段落で具体化されているので、そちらで書くことにします。第3文は具体例なので省くことにします。8点満点で、各区分4点として減

点法で採点します。

[**要約例**] Large numbers of children in Africa have no access to education.
「アフリカでは多くの子どもたちは教育を受けられない」

第2段落

　　These areas — often remote — lack both schools and teachers, and a UN assessment notes that even when teachers are available, they are often poorly trained or not trained at all. This leaves children with no choice but to become manual laborers early in life. This results in a net loss for national and regional development since an educated workforce is necessary for industrialization and modernization. In fact, even basic economic advancement requires a workforce with at least an elementary level of schooling.

　　こうした地域は人里離れたところにあることが多いが、学校も教師も不足しており、国連の評価では、教師がいても、きちんとした訓練を受けていなかったり、まったく訓練を受けていなかったりすることが多いと指摘されている。このため、子どもたちは人生の早い段階で肉体労働者になるという選択肢しか残されていない。産業化と近代化には教育を受けた労働力が必要であるため、これは国や地域の発展にとって最終的には損失となる。さらに言えば、最少限の経済発展でさえ、少なくとも初等レベルの学校教育を受けた労働力が必要なのである。

語彙リスト

☐ **4.**	asséssment	名	評価
☐ **5.**	leave A with B	熟	A に B を残す
☐ **6.**	no choice but to (V)	熟	V 以外の選択肢がないこと
☐ **7.**	mánual làborer	名	肉体労働者
☐ **8.**	nèt lóss	名	純損失、最終的な損失
☐ **9.**	indùstrializátion	名	産業化
☐ **10.**	mòdernizátion	名	近代化

解説と要旨

　　第1文は❶「学校と訓練された教師が不足している」という内容です。第2～4文には、第1文の結果が述べられています。それらは❷「子どもが労働者になり」❸「産業化と近代化には、少なくとも初等レベルの教育を受けた労働者が必要なので、この地域が発展しない」ということです。「この地域が発展しない」は、解答以外にはthese areas remain underdeveloped「この地域は未開発のままになる」などとします。9点満点で、各区分3点として減点法で採点します。

[要約例] … due to a lack of schools and trained teachers. This results in child labor and hinders national and regional development, since economic progress requires a workforce with a basic level of education.

「(これは) 学校や訓練を受けた教師の不足が原因である。その結果、児童労働を生み出し、国と地域の発展を妨げている。なぜなら、経済発展には、基本的な教育を受けた労働力が必要だからだ」

第3段落

In parts of Africa, material educational challenges are exacerbated by gender inequalities. As in much of the developing world, there is a strong preference for boys among many African families, and if they have resources to spend on education, boys will usually receive that education instead of girls: in Niger, 70% of poor girls receive no education at all, meaning that they can contribute almost nothing to the national economy. Mothers without formal education are also an issue. UNESCO's research indicates that the first 1,000 days of life are critical for a child's physical, mental, and educational growth, including early literacy, numeracy and social skills. However, poorly educated mothers are unable to provide these skills. This is therefore a crucial problem to be addressed, considering that providing women with educational opportunities brings great returns to the state, educated girls significantly increase the country's GDP and educated mothers are able to raise healthier children.

アフリカの一部では、男女間の不平等によって、教育面における深刻な問題が悪化している。発展途上国の多くにおいてと同様、アフリカの多くの家庭では男児を好む傾向が強く、教育に費やす資源があれば、女児ではなく男児が教育を受けるのが普通である。ニジェールでは、貧困層の女児の70％がまったく教育を受けておらず、これは彼女らが国家の経済にほとんど貢献できないことを意味する。正式な教育を受けていない母親も問題である。ユネスコの調査によると、生まれてから最初の1,000日間は、子どもの身体的、精神的、教育的成長にとって非常に重要であり、これには初期の読み書き能力、計算能力、社会的スキルも含まれる。しかし、教育水準の低い母親は、こうしたスキルを提供することができない。したがって、女性に教育の機会を与えることが国家に大きな見返りをもたらし、教育を受けた女児は国のGDPを大幅に拡大し、教育を受けた母親はより健康な子どもを育てることができることを考慮すれば、これは対処すべき極めて深刻な問題なのである。

☐ **11.**	matérial	形	深刻な、重要な
☐ **12.**	exácerbàte ～	動	～を悪化させる
☐ **13.**	contríbute A to B	熟	A を B に提供する
☐ **14.**	crítical	形	極めて重要な ※crisis の形容詞形。
☐ **15.**	crúcial	形	極めて重要な
			※cross「十字架」と同系語。

解説と要旨

　第1文は、❶「アフリカにおける男女間の不平等が、事態を悪化させている」という内容です。exacerbate ～「～を悪化させる」は、類義語の aggravate や compound で置き換えるか、簡単に make ～ worse とすればよいでしょう。第2文は❷「女児より男児に教育費用をかける傾向があり、女児が国家の経済にほとんど貢献できないということを意味する」という内容を書きます。後半の「女児が国家の経済にほとんど貢献できないということを意味する」は、次の文にも含まれるのでなくてもよいでしょう。第3～5文は、❸「（女性に教育の機会を与えることは、国家に大きな見返りをもたらし、）教育を受けた女児は国の GDP を大幅に拡大し」、❹「教育を受けた母親はより健康な子どもを育てることができる」という内容が書ければ OK です。「女性に教育の機会を与えることは、国家に大きな見返りをもたらし」は、なくても可とします。8点満点で、各区分2点として減点法で採点します。

[要約例] Gender disparities also persist in African education, with limited early childhood education access for girls and a gender gap in school enrollment, influenced by African society's prioritizing the education of boys over that of girls. However, expanding educational opportunities for girls and women has great economic and family health benefits. Specifically, educated girls can boost the GDP, while educated women can ensure their family health.

　「アフリカの教育においても男女格差は根強く、女子の教育よりも男子の教育を優遇するアフリカ社会の影響により、女子が初等教育を受ける機会は限られており、就学における男女格差がある。しかし、女子や女性の教育機会を拡大することは、経済面でも、家族の健康面でも大きなメリットがある。具体的には、教育を受けた女子は GDP を増大させ、教育を受けた女性は家族の健康を守ることができる」

STEP 2
モニター答案でポイントをつかむ

[モニター答案例1]［11 / 25点］

Many children in Africa still cannot receive an education and many of them work instead of studying mainly because they have no other choices. There are few teachers who are educated <u>and</u> schools in these areas, which <u>leads children to</u>
               ✖ →or：−1点   ✖ →means that children：−2点

have to become manual laborers. Moreover, this makes it difficult ✖ <u>to</u> develop
                                                ヌケ→for these areas：−2点

<u>these countries</u> because <u>the</u> economic development requires <u>those who at least</u>
✖ →トル：−1点   ✖ →トル：−1点   ✖ → people who have at least graduated：−3点

<u>graduate</u> from elementary school. Gender inequalities also make the educational problems worse. The number of boys going to school is much larger than that of girls. Government should try to provide educational opportunities to women because this would be beneficial for women and the nations.   (108 words)

[**内容点**] 第1段落は❶❷ともにOK。第2段落の❶❷❸とも、文法的には難があるが、内容面はOK。第3段落の❶はOK。❷は「女子の教育よりも男子の教育を優遇する社会の影響を受けている」がヌケで−1点。❸❹が不十分で−3点。以上、−4点。
[**文法点**] −10点。本文ではlack A and Bだが、否定文ではA or Bになることに注意したい。
[**総評**] まずまずの出来である。時制のミスがあるので、今後は時制に注意を払うようにすればよいだろう。

1
級

[モニター答案例2]［4 / 25点］

Millions of children ✖ <u>do</u> not have access to education. Instead of studying,
ヌケ→in West and Central Africa：内容点で減点

04

189

they work in various fields. This is because there are few options they can choose.

There are few schools and teachers. Also, those teachers are hardly trained.
✕ →or：−1点   ✕ untrained or insufficiently trained：−3点

Because of this, they choose to become manual labor. Their countries do not
✕ →laborers：−1点

develop because they need labor with at least elementary levels of education. In

parts of Africa, the educational problems get worse due to gender inequality and

parents tend to spend more money on their sons than on their daughters. Thus,

many girls are not educated. Poorly educated women cannot provide ✕ skills to
ヌケ→a healthy upbringing or：−3点

their children, so giving women educational opportunities benefit a lot. (114 words)
✕ →would greatly benefit these countries：−3点

［**内容点**］語数オーバーで−4点。第1段落の❶は「アフリカ」のヌケで−2点。❷は
OK。第2段落は、❶❷❸とも文法面では難があるが、内容面はOK。第3段落は、❶
はOK。❷は「女子の教育よりも男子の教育を優遇する社会の影響を受けている」の
ヌケで−1点。❸❹が不十分で−3点。以上、−10点。

［**文法点**］−11点。

［**総評**］不注意なミスが散見される。隅々まで気を配って書くこと。

STEP 3
ネイティブスピーカーの解答に学ぶ

Millions of children in West and Central Africa are deprived of
education, forced into labor due to a severe lack of schooling options.
Remote areas suffer from insufficient facilities and poorly trained
teachers. This perpetuates a cycle of manual labor by children, and
hinders national and regional development. Gender biases prevalent in

African society exacerbate the problem. Girls receive significantly less access to education, which negatively affects both their individual prospects and local economies. Investing in women's education yields pronounced returns, improving infant health and contributing to economic growth. This underscores the vital role of education in fostering development on this continent.

(102 words)

西アフリカと中央アフリカでは、学校教育の選択肢が極端に不足しているために何百万人もの子どもたちが教育を奪われ、労働を強いられている。遠隔地では不十分な施設と訓練不足の教師に苦しめられている。このことが、児童肉体労働の連鎖を永続させ、国や地域の発展を妨げている。アフリカ社会に蔓延する性差別が、この問題をさらに悪化させている。女子は教育を受ける機会が著しく少なく、そのことが個人の将来性と地域経済の両方に悪影響を及ぼす。女性の教育への投資は、乳幼児の健康を改善し、経済成長に貢献するなど、顕著な見返りをもたらす。それを考えれば、この大陸の開発を促進する上で、教育が極めて重要な役割を担っていることは明白だ。

語彙リスト

☐ **1.**	hínder ～	動	～を妨げる
☐ **2.**	perpétuate a cycle	熟	連鎖を永続させる
☐ **3.**	génder bìas	名	性差別
☐ **4.**	pronóunced	形	顕著な
☐ **5.**	próspect	名	展望
☐ **6.**	únderscòre ～	動	～を強調する、明白にする

1級

04

解 答 例

Venezuela was once among the richest countries in the world in terms of oil reserves and accepted many refugees. However, it is currently facing the second most serious humanitarian crisis in the world, with increasing poverty and insecurity. Consequently, over 7 million people have been forced to flee the country over the past several years. The country's economic downturn was caused by government misrule and corruption, and plummeting oil prices. Moreover, hyperinflation made the situation worse, leading to widespread violence and shortages of food and basic products. Millions of Venezuelan refugees fled to neighboring countries. However, despite the crisis, an increasing number of refugees are returning to their homeland.

(109 words)

　ベネズエラはかつて世界有数の石油埋蔵量を誇る豊かな国であり、多くの難民を受け入れていた。しかし、現在ベネズエラは世界で2番目に深刻な人道危機に直面しており、貧困と治安が悪化している。そのため、過去数年にわたり700万人以上の人々が国外脱出を余儀なくされてきた。この国の経済の低迷を引き起こしたのは、政府の失政と汚職、それに原油価格の急落である。さらに、ハイパーインフレが状況を悪化させ、暴力が蔓延し、食糧や必需品の不足という事態になった。数百万人のベネズエラ難民が近隣諸国へ逃げた。しかし、危機的状況にもかかわらず、母国に戻る難民が増加している。

STEP 1
問題文の要点をつかむ

第1段落

Venezuela was once known as one of the great resort areas of the Caribbean and had some of the largest oil reserves in the world. Also, it used to be a rich country that accepted refugees from many nations. However, the humanitarian crisis in Venezuela has escalated to become the second largest in the world, following the long-standing conflict in Syria, making it the largest refugee crisis in South America. Since 2014, more than 7.3 million Venezuelans have left the country, with 20 percent of the population having departed, due to poverty and worsening security situations. In fact, as of September 2023, there were 7.7 million refugees and migrants forced to flee their homes.

ベネズエラはかつてカリブ海の一大リゾート地として知られ、世界有数の石油埋蔵量を誇っていた。また、かつては多くの国から難民を受け入れる豊かな国でもあった。しかし、ベネズエラで人道危機がエスカレートし、長年のシリア紛争に次ぐ世界第2位の規模となり、南米最大の難民危機となっている。2014年以降、730万人以上のベネズエラ人が貧困と治安悪化により国外に流出したが、これは人口の20%が国外に流出したことになる。実際、2023年9月の時点で、故郷を追われた難民や移民は770万人に上る。

語彙リスト

□ **1.**	the Caríbbean	名	カリブ海
□ **2.**	òil resérve	名	石油埋蔵量
□ **3.**	rèfugée	名	難民
□ **4.**	humànitárian crìsis	名	人道危機
□ **5.**	éscalàte to (V)	熟	エスカレートして〜する
□ **6.**	lóng-stánding	形	長期の
□ **7.**	with 〜 having ...		※独立分詞構文

□ **8.**	depárt	動	出て行く
□ **9.**	wórsening	形	悪化する
□ **10.**	as of（日付）	熟	〜現在で
□ **11.**	flee 〜	動	〜から逃げる

※活用はflee - fled - fled

解説と要旨

　第1〜2文は❶「ベネズエラはかつて世界有数の石油埋蔵量を誇る豊かな国であり」、❷「多くの難民を受け入れてきた」とします。「世界有数の石油埋蔵量」「豊かな国」「多くの難民の受け入れ」というポイントは外せません。「一大リゾート地」は、「豊かだ」の中にその意味は含まれており、この文全体では大きな意味をもたないので省いてよいでしょう。第3文以降は、❸「ベネズエラは世界で2番目に深刻な人道危機に直面しており、貧困と治安が悪化している」、❹「そのため、数年前から700万人以上の人々が国外脱出を余儀なくされてきた」とします。「世界で2番目に深刻な人道危機に直面」「貧困と治安の悪化」「700万人以上が国外脱出」というポイントは外せません。8点満点で、各区分2点として減点法で採点します。

[要約例] Venezuela was once among the richest countries in the world in terms of oil reserves and accepted many refugees. However, it is currently facing the second most serious humanitarian crisis in the world, with increasing poverty and insecurity. Consequently, over 7 million people have been forced to flee the country over the past several years.

　「ベネズエラはかつて世界有数の石油埋蔵量を誇る豊かな国であり、多くの難民を受け入れていた。しかし、現在ベネズエラは世界で2番目に深刻な人道危機に直面しており、貧困と治安が悪化している。そのため、過去数年にわたり700万人以上の人々が国外脱出を余儀なくされてきた」

第 2 段 落

　Years of economic mismanagement and corruption under former president, Hugo Chávez played a major role in the substantial reduction of oil production and profits. Furthermore, the drop in global oil prices in 2014 led to a rapid economic decline. Consequently, Venezuela has been suffering from hyperinflation since the end of 2017, when the inflation rate rose to a frightening 1.3 million percent per year. As a result, people in Venezuela could not survive, and many, including many in the indigenous population, were compelled to leave for other countries. The loss of social order has led to widespread violence and a declining economic state, resulting in shortages of food, clothing, medicine, and other necessities.

ウゴ・チャベス前大統領の下での長年の経済失政と汚職が主な原因となり、石油の生産と利益が大幅に減少した。さらに、2014年の世界的な原油価格の下落は、急速な経済衰退につながった。その結果、ベネズエラは2017年末からハイパーインフレに見舞われ、インフレ率が年間130万％という恐ろしい数字にまで上昇した。その結果、ベネズエラの人々は生きていくことができなくなり、先住民族を含む多くの人々が他国への移住を余儀なくされた。社会秩序が失われたことで、暴力が蔓延して、経済状態が悪化し、その結果、食糧、衣料、医薬品、その他の必需品が不足するようになった。

語彙リスト

☐ **12.**	mìsmánagement	名	失政、ずさんな管理 [経営]
☐ **13.**	corrúption	名	汚職
☐ **14.**	substántial	形	かなりの
☐ **15.**	económic decline	名	経済の衰退
☐ **16.**	hỳperinflátion	名	ハイパーインフレ
☐ **17.**	indígenous populàtion	名	先住民族
☐ **18.**	be compélled to (V)	熟	〜を余儀なくされる
☐ **19.**	sócial òrder	名	社会秩序
☐ **20.**	shórtage	名	不足

解説と要旨

この段落は第1段落の背景について述べられています。第1〜2文は❶「この国の経済の低迷を引き起こしたのは、政府の失政と汚職、それに原油価格の急落である」という内容であり、「政府の失政と汚職」「原油価格の急落」という2つのポイントは外せません。第3〜5文は、❷「さらに、ハイパーインフレは状況を悪化させ」、❸「暴力が蔓延し、食糧や必需品の不足を引き起こした」がポイントです。ここでは「ハイパーインフレによる状況の悪化」「暴力の蔓延」「食糧や必需品の不足」が重要です。9点満点で、各区分3点として減点法で採点します。

[**要約例**] The country's economic downturn was caused by government misrule and corruption, and plummeting oil prices. Moreover, hyperinflation made the situation worse, leading to widespread violence and shortages of food and basic products.

「この国の経済の低迷を引き起こしたのは、政府の失政と汚職、それに原油価格の急落である。さらに、ハイパーインフレが状況を悪化させ、暴力が蔓延し、食糧や必需品の不足という事態になった」

第3段落

Latin American countries, such as Colombia, Peru, and Ecuador, are hosting many Venezuelan refugees. Colombia, in particular, has become home to the highest number of them, with a minimum of 2.9 million refugees. Despite the ongoing economic crisis, many of the Venezuelan refugees have expressed a desire to return home. Recently, an increasing number of people have decided to return to their homeland.

コロンビア、ペルー、エクアドルなどのラテンアメリカ諸国は、多くのベネズエラ難民を受け入れている。特にコロンビアはその数が最も多く、少なくとも290万人の難民を受け入れている。経済危機が続いているにもかかわらず、多くの難民が帰国を希望している。最近では、母国への帰国を決断する人が増えている。

語彙リスト

☐ **21.** óngòing   形 現在進行中の

解説と要旨

第1～2文は❶「近隣諸国は数百万人のベネズエラ難民を受け入れている」となります。近隣諸国の具体的な国名を入れる余裕はないでしょう。第3～4文は❷「しかし、危機的状況にもかかわらず、母国に戻る者が増加している」とすればよいでしょう。8点満点で、各区分4点として減点法で採点します。

[要 約 例] Millions of Venezuelan refugees fled to neighboring countries. However, despite the crisis, an increasing number of refugees are returning to their homeland.

「数百万人のベネズエラ難民が近隣諸国へ逃げた。しかし、危機的状況にもかかわらず、母国に戻る難民が増加している」

STEP 2
モニター答案でポイントをつかむ

［**モニター答案例1**］［**2 / 25点**］

In the past, thanks to its resort areas and oil profits, Venezuela was so rich that

✗ →profits from its resort areas and oil →−2点

it could accept a lot of refugees. However, there has been the great humanitarian

△ →numerous：減点なし　　　　　　　　　　　✗ →a：−1点

crisis in Venezuela since 2014, because of the reduction of the production of oil and

✗ →there：−1点　　　　　✗ →a reduction in：−1点

the decline of oil prices. Since then, a lot of people has emigrated from it due to

✗ →a decline in：−2点　　△ →a large number of：減点なし　　✗ →have：−1点

poverty and the bad security situations. Moreover, there has been hyperinflation

✗ →insecurity：−2点

since 2017. However, while the situation is still worse, more and more Venezuelans

have decided to return there recently.　　　　　　　　　　　　　　(92 words)

［**内容点**］第1段落❶については「世界有数の石油埋蔵量」とは書かれていないが可とする。❷もOK。❸は「世界で2番目に深刻な」がヌケで−1点。「貧困と治安の悪化」は解答の後半に書かれているので可とする。❹が不十分で−1点。第2段落は、❶の「政府の失政」「汚職」がヌケで−3点。❷が不十分で−1点。❸がヌケで−3点。第3段落は❶がヌケで−4点。❷はOK。以上、−13点。
［**文法点**］−10点。
［**総評**］1級レベルのエッセーでは、口語体の語句は極力使わないようにしたい。よって、a lot of ～「たくさんの～」は避けること。また「～における増加・減少」の「～における」はinを使うことにも注意したい。

［**モニター答案例2**］［**14 / 25点**］

In the past, thanks to oil production, Venezuela used to be a rich country and many people visited it on their vacation. Therefore, Venezuela had accepted

✕ →トル：−2点

✕ refugees from other countries. However, the political corruption and the drop in

ヌケ→many：−1点

global oil prices led ✕ the economic crisis of Venezuela. Due to the economic

ヌケ→to：−2点

crisis, people in Venezuela have been suffering from violence and the shortages of

necessities. Thus, they have been forced to leave their country. They went to other

Latin American countries as refugees. Although the situation of Venezuela has not

been improved, more and more Venezuelan refugees are returning to Venezuela

these days. (103 words)

[**内容点**] 第1段落の❶については「世界有数の石油埋蔵量を誇る」とは書かれていないが可とする。❷はOK。❸が不十分で−1点。❹が不十分で−1点。第2段落の❶は「失政」がヌケで−1点。❷がヌケで−3点。❸はOK。第3段落の❶は可とする。❷はOK。以上、−6点。

[**文法点**] −5点。

[**総評**] 第1文と第2文は、原因・結果の関係にはない。つまり、「富を持った観光国」が必ずしも「難民を受け入れる」ということにはならないからだ。よってThereforeを使うのはおかしい。論理関係には十分に気をつけないといけない。

STEP 3
ネイティブスピーカーの解答に学ぶ

模範解答

Once famous for its resorts and abundant oil reserves, Venezuela now faces the world's second-largest humanitarian crisis. Since 2014, over 7.3 million Venezuelans have fled their homeland, with a fifth of the population driven out by poverty and instability. Economic mismanagement and corruption, especially under Hugo Chávez, led to plummeting oil production and profits, exacerbated by a 2014 drop in global oil prices. Hyperinflation soared to 1.3 million percent annually by 2017, causing widespread deprivation and violence. Nations such as Peru and Ecuador and especially Colombia are currently home to millions of Venezuelan refugees. Despite challenges, some are returning home amid the crisis.

(103 words)

かつてリゾート地と豊富な石油埋蔵量で有名だったベネズエラは、いまや世界で2番目に大きな人道危機に直面している。2014年以来、730万人以上のベネズエラ人が祖国を逃れ、人口の5分の1が貧困と不安定な情勢によって国外に追いやられた。特にウゴ・チャベス政権下での経済失政と汚職は、石油の生産量と利益の激減につながり、2014年の世界的な原油価格の下落によって悪化した。ハイパーインフレは2017年までに年間130万％まで高騰し、広範な必需品不足と暴力を引き起こした。ペルー、エクアドル、特にコロンビアなどの国々には、現在何百万ものベネズエラ難民が住んでいる。困難にもかかわらず、危機の中で帰国する人もいる。

語彙リスト

☐ **1.** soar　　　　　　　　　　　**動** 高騰する

☐ **2.** plúmmet　　　　　　　　　 **動** 急落する

1級

05

著者

竹岡 広信
HIRONOBU TAKEOKA

学研プライムゼミ特任講師、駿台予備学校講師、竹岡塾主宰。「先生のおかげで英語が克服できた」と多くの東大合格者が信頼を寄せるカリスマ英語講師。「日本の英語教育をよくしたい」という情熱を凝縮した講義は受験生を魅了し、数多くの生徒を難関大学の合格へと導き続けている。『竹岡の英文法・語法ULTIMATE 究極の600題』（Gakken）、『改訂新版 ドラゴン・イングリッシュ基本英文100』（講談社）、『決定版 竹岡広信の英作文が面白いほど書ける本』（KADOKAWA）などの大学受験参考書のベストセラーを多く世に送り出している。40年来の英検®ファンを自負し、英検®を熟知していることでも有名。『竹岡の英検®準1級マスター』（監・著、教学社）、『最短合格! 英検®準1級 リーディング問題完全制覇』（監修、ジャパンタイムズ）などの英検®対策書も多く手がけている。

制作スタッフ

問題英文作成	株式会社CPI Japan、日本アイアール株式会社
編集協力	日本アイアール株式会社、今居美月、石川道子、挙市玲子
模範解答作成	Stephen Richmond
英文校閲	Kathryn A. Craft
ブックデザイン	chichols

読者アンケートのお願い

この度は弊社商品をお買い上げいただき、誠にありがとうございます。本書に関するアンケートにご協力ください。右下の二次元コードから、アンケートフォームにアクセスすることができます。ご協力いただいた方のなかから抽選でギフト券（500円分）をプレゼントさせていただきます

アンケート番号　305946

※アンケートは予告なく終了する場合がございます。

英検®合格
のための

要約問題
予想問題集
問題編

もくじ

英検®は、公益財団法人 日本英語検定協会の登録商標です。このコンテンツは、公益財団法人 日本英語検定協会の承認や推奨、その他の検討を受けたものではありません。

- 以下の英文を読んで、その内容を英語で要約し、解答欄に記入しなさい。
- 語数の目安は45語〜55語です。
- 解答欄の外に書かれたものは採点されません。
- 解答が英文の要約になっていないと判断された場合は、0点と採点されることがあります。英文をよく読んでから答えてください。

Students used to use either paper or electronic dictionaries when they studied a foreign language, but nowadays many do not use either option. Instead, they use online dictionaries.

What are the reasons for this? Online dictionaries are most accessible because most students have a smartphone and they can easily access the Internet through it. Online dictionaries are much lighter and cheaper than the other two. Students can listen to the proper pronunciation of words, too.

Needless to say, there are some disadvantages to online dictionaries as well. Depending on the Wi-Fi connection, the students may not be able to access them. Most importantly, if the students often use online dictionaries, they will become dependent on them and no longer voluntarily learn new words. They may get distracted by phone calls, emails, videos, and entertainment apps. As a result, they may not be able to focus on studying.

解 答 欄

5

10

15

- 以下の英文を読んで、その内容を英語で要約し、解答欄に記入しなさい。
- 語数の目安は45語～55語です。
- 解答欄の外に書かれたものは採点されません。
- 解答が英文の要約になっていないと判断された場合は、0点と採点されることがあります。英文をよく読んでから答えてください。

One of the greatest things about public libraries is that they are open to all. No special degree or license is required to enter a public library. However, with the rise of technology, the importance of their existence is being questioned.

Why should libraries be saved? The internet certainly provides all the information we need, but the experience we get when we spend time in a library is not one we can get elsewhere. Some libraries are also needed for preserving old books and editions that cannot be found online.

On the other hand, there are some negative aspects of libraries. When we borrow a book from a library, we must return it within a set period. Furthermore, many people do not feel that they have to return books in perfect condition. Libraries have also seen cases where pages of books are found to be damaged or marked.

解答欄

5

10

15

- 以下の英文を読んで、その内容を英語で要約し、解答欄に記入しなさい。
- 語数の目安は45語〜55語です。
- 解答欄の外に書かれたものは採点されません。
- 解答が英文の要約になっていないと判断された場合は、0点と採点されることがあります。英文をよく読んでから答えてください。

A "gap year" is a period of time off from formal schooling taken by students to gain experience through activities such as study abroad, internships, and volunteer work before entering university or during university, and occasionally after graduation until starting a job.

What can students gain through this experience? A gap year provides the opportunity for students to learn what they could not in the classroom. For instance, they can learn about various cultures and acquire valuable skills. In addition, students who have experienced a gap year have higher motivation and planning ability after entering school compared to students who have not.

In Japan, this system was unfamiliar until now, but now some universities allow this period before and immediately after entering the university to support students. It is hoped that more universities in Japan will become aware of the benefits of this system and adopt it.

解 答 欄

2
級

03

5

10

15

Space exploration has long been a worldwide effort to explore the potential of the universe. When many people hear the term "space exploration," they think of rocket launches, space stations, and so on. However, what exactly is being done is probably not well known to most people.

What are the advantages of space exploration? First of all, it will contribute to the advancement of scientific knowledge and technology. Finding the origins of the universe will improve not only knowledge but also technology. In addition, it will lead to the creation of industries and jobs. Many people may work in fields we have never dreamed of. Furthermore, working on space development may help solve food shortages, population problems, and other issues.

However, there is one big disadvantage of space exploration. Space research involves a long research period, and as a result, it requires a large amount of money. Furthermore, even if huge amounts of public funds are used, the results may not be as expected.

解 答 欄

5

10

15

● 以下の英文を読んで、その内容を英語で要約し、解答欄に記入しなさい。
● 語数の目安は45語～55語です。
● 解答欄の外に書かれたものは採点されません。
● 解答が英文の要約になっていないと判断された場合は、0点と採点されること
  があります。英文をよく読んでから答えてください。

A survey released in 2021 revealed that 51.3% of young adults had a driver's license and 14.4% owned their own car. More than 90% of those between the ages of 35 and 59 had a driver's license, so compared to this group, fewer people in the younger generation had a license.

What are the reasons for this trend? Some people say that it takes a lot of time to obtain a car license. Others say the cost of purchasing and repairing a car is high. Needless to say, finding a parking space is another problem.

Certainly, many people may not need a license for their daily commute to work or school. However, with a driver's license and a car, they can often shorten their commute, especially if they know how to avoid busy roads and highways. Another benefit is that a license can be used as a form of identification.

解答欄

5

10

15

● 以下の英文を読んで、その内容を英語で要約し、解答欄に記入しなさい。
● 語数の目安は45語〜55語です。
● 解答欄の外に書かれたものは採点されません。
● 解答が英文の要約になっていないと判断された場合は、0点と採点されることがあります。英文をよく読んでから答えてください。

According to a recent survey of Japanese university students, more than 40% of them either rent a house or apartment. It seems that many students, although less than half, live alone after entering university.

What are the advantages of living alone? The greatest advantage is that you can live freely without anyone interfering in your life. You do not have to adjust to your family's lifestyle or worry about what time you will be home. Even on holidays, nobody wakes you up, so you may sleep longer.

However, there are some disadvantages. One of them is that you will need to do all the housework by yourself. Doing housework surely improves your life skills, but it can be stressful because nobody helps you with it. Also, when you go home, there is no one to talk to, so you may feel lonely.

解 答 欄

5

10

15

- 以下の英文を読んで、その内容を<u>英語で要約</u>し、解答欄に記入しなさい。
- 語数の目安は45語〜55語です。
- <u>解答欄の外に書かれたものは採点されません。</u>
- 解答が英文の要約になっていないと判断された場合は、<u>0点と採点されること</u><u>があります</u>。英文をよく読んでから答えてください。

In Japan, while more than 90% of all age groups use social networking sites, the highest rate of social media use was among high school students. Of all these sites, messaging apps are the most widely used by them.

Why do so many people use social media? The biggest advantage of it is that it provides them with many ways to connect with others. Also, they can get the information they want to get in a short time, which is very convenient.

Despite these advantages, you have to be careful because not all information on social media is correct. Some of it may be false information. Furthermore, using social media can cause anxiety, depression, and other health problems. Finally, since anyone can read social media posts, posting personal information, such as where you live or when you will be away from home, can put you at risk.

解 答 欄

5

10

15

● 以下の英文を読んで、その内容を英語で要約し、解答欄に記入しなさい。

● 語数の目安は45語〜55語です。

● 解答欄の外に書かれたものは採点されません。

● 解答が英文の要約になっていないと判断された場合は、0点と採点されること
があります。英文をよく読んでから答えてください。

Nowadays, when taking notes, more people use computers than write by hand. However, according to a research team from a university in Norway, the brain was more active when subjects wrote by hand than when they typed on a keyboard.

What are the advantages of writing by hand? One advantage of it is that taking notes with paper and pen is very useful when studying. It may not be as fast as typing on a computer, but you stay focused while writing notes by hand. Also, the information is easier to remember because your fingers are not moving on their own without thinking as they do when you type.

However, handwriting also has some disadvantages. One of the problems is that paper memos are easy to lose. Another one is that memos are difficult to share with others. It is also possible that your handwriting is so poor that nobody else can read it.

解 答 欄

5

10

15

- 以下の英文を読んで、その内容を<u>英語で要約</u>し、解答欄に記入しなさい。
- 語数の目安は45語〜55語です。
- 解答欄の外に書かれたものは採点されません。
- 解答が英文の要約になっていないと判断された場合は、<u>0点と採点されること</u><u>があります</u>。英文をよく読んでから答えてください。

Machine translation, which uses computers to perform translation, is said to have improved in accuracy in recent years. And it is expected that machine translation will be used by more companies. Machine translation itself has existed for some time. However, the results were not very accurate and were not suitable for serious business use.

How will machine translation benefit businesses and language learning? The biggest advantage is the short time required for translation. With machine translation, a simple document can be translated in a few seconds. This allows you to finish the task in a shorter time. This also means that you can lower translation costs.

On the other hand, there are also some problems. Communication often involves cultural backgrounds that do not necessarily appear in the texts themselves. Unlike human translators, machines lack awareness of the unstated cultural assumptions that communication between countries requires, so the translations can be wrong.

解 答 欄

5

10

15

- 以下の英文を読んで、その内容を英語で要約し、解答欄に記入しなさい。
- 語数の目安は45語〜55語です。
- 解答欄の外に書かれたものは採点されません。
- 解答が英文の要約になっていないと判断された場合は、0点と採点されることがあります。英文をよく読んでから答えてください。

Electric kick scooters, or electric kickboards are gradually changing the way people get around every day around the world. Some people buy gasoline-powered cars and motorcycles, but these scooters are becoming more popular due to their convenience and other reasons.

What kind of benefits do the electric kickboards have? Since they are powered by electricity, they are less harmful to the environment than gas-powered vehicles. In addition, their motors produce very little noise compared to engines. Furthermore, they are more compact than ordinary bicycles, so they can be easily stored and carried around.

One weak point is they are capable of reaching speeds of more than 30 mph and can be very dangerous. In fact, accidents involving them have resulted in death. Also, since they have no roof, they cannot be used on rainy days. Since they have no basket, they cannot carry large items. Finally, they are not vehicles suitable for long-distance travel because they are smaller than gasoline-powered motorbikes.

2
級

5

10

10

15

- Instructions: Read the article below and summarize it in your own words as far as possible in English.
- Suggested length: 60-70 words
- Write your summary in the space provided on your answer sheet. Any writing outside the space will not be graded.

In 2013, public transportation became free in Tallinn, the capital of Estonia. Before that, free public transportation initiatives had been implemented only in relatively small municipalities and never in a capital city. Under the initiative, only registered residents can purchase a "green card" for two euros, and with that, all buses, streetcars, and trolleybuses in the city are free of charge.

These initiatives were expected to bring benefits, such as increased tax revenues due to a population increase for free rides, reduced equipment costs for railway companies, contributing to a better environment due to reduced number of cars, and improved mobility for low-income people.

According to a 2014 survey, it is true that the number of times Tallinn residents walked on foot decreased by 40%. However, the number of times they traveled by car decreased by only 5%. Apparently, the effect on gas emissions was not as large as had been expected. And of course, this does not seem to be suitable for every city. For example, in Paris, France, there are many people who oppose the idea of free fares, believing that it would simply lead to a reduction in fare revenues, which would ultimately increase the burden on taxpayers.

解答欄

		5
		<div style="text-align:center">準 1 級 01</div>
		10
		15
		20

- **Instructions: Read the article below and summarize it in your own words as far as possible in English.**
- **Suggested length: 60-70 words**
- **Write your summary in the space provided on your answer sheet. <u>Any writing outside the space will not be graded.</u>**

Portugal followed the example of Belgium and the United Kingdom by announcing the introduction of a four-day workweek on a trial basis. Debate over the four-day workweek has been heating up thanks to the virus outbreak, which prompted workers and employers to rethink the importance of workplace flexibility and benefits.

Belgium became the first European country to legalize a four-day workweek. In February 2022, Belgian employees who would normally work five days a week won the right to a four-day workweek without a cut in pay. Belgian Prime Minister Alexander De Croo said the changes should help Belgians find it easier to combine their family lives and careers, creating a more dynamic economy.

However, the idea of a four-day workweek is not popular with everyone. For instance, some full-time employees, who already work full days, are opposed to the idea of working even longer hours on the days they work, saying that working days may be reduced, but they will be condensed into fewer days. What's more, those who take shifts complain that they will not be able to take advantage of the flexibility.

解 答 欄

5

準
1
級

02

10

15

20

- Instructions: Read the article below and summarize it in your own words as far as possible in English.
- Suggested length: 60-70 words
- Write your summary in the space provided on your answer sheet. Any writing outside the space will not be graded.

In recent years, unstaffed convenience stores have become common in Asian countries, such as China, Japan, and Singapore. In an unstaffed convenience store, machines perform basic operations in the store, and there are no store clerks.

At unstaffed convenience stores, customers simply swipe their mobile phones to enter, select and pick up items, pay using self-service registers, and leave. That way, people can save a lot of time. The benefits to the shop are that labor costs are greatly reduced. Cutting-edge technology makes it easier to manage products, and it is possible to monitor the purchase, inventory, and sales status of products.

Despite these advantages, there are a lot of problems to overcome as well. A large amount of money is required for the introduction of equipment and technology. Not only are there food hygiene and safety issues, but also there is the issue of cleanliness. There may be dust on the product shelves, or when people enter the store from outside on a rainy day, the floor may get dirty. These are the issues that unstaffed convenience stores have to deal with.

解 答 欄

- Instructions: Read the article below and summarize it in your own words as far as possible in English.
- Suggested length: 60-70 words
- Write your summary in the space provided on your answer sheet. Any writing outside the space will not be graded.

The Minimum Legal Drinking Age (MLDA) is 21 in all 50 states in the United States, but 18 is the "age of majority" in 47 of the 50 states, allowing people to have the rights and responsibilities of an adult. Each state sets its own age of majority, which often coincides with the age at which one can vote, sign contracts, get married, and so on. Therefore, there have been a lot of discussions about whether setting the MLDA at 21 is fair and effective.

As for African countries, the age at which people can buy alcohol is around 18 years old. However, in Ethiopia, people can buy alcohol at the age of 15, and in Zimbabwe at the age of 16. Algeria allows 18-year-olds to buy alcohol, but few shops sell it because it is a Muslim country.

The main reasons for opposing the lowering of the drinking age in the U.S. are concerns that underage drinking may have serious effects on brain function and that increased underage drinking may lead to more traffic accidents and deaths.

解 答 欄

5

準
1
級

10

04

15

20

- **Instructions: Read the article below and summarize it in your own words as far as possible in English.**
- **Suggested length: 60-70 words**
- **Write your summary in the space provided on your answer sheet. Any writing outside the space will not be graded.**

Clothing rental subscription is a service that allows you to rent various items for a monthly fee. There are different rental methods depending on the number of items delivered, and there are plans where you can choose your favorite items, and plans where you receive coordinated outfits selected by a stylist. In the United States, as of 2020, over 11 million users have used this service. And the US clothing rental market could reach $4.4 billion by 2028.

With a subscription service, you can rent unique designer items for a low price. This cuts down on the number of items you buy and wear only once and throw away. The amount of clothing waste in Japan alone exceeds 500,000 tons annually, so such a service would be beneficial to the environment.

On the other hand, the disadvantage of a clothing rental subscription is that you cannot try the items on in advance. Nor can you pick up the actual item and touch it. You can only check the images and information posted, and there may be some discrepancies. Moreover, most of the products handled by the clothing subscription service are not new.

解 答 欄

5

10

15

20

準1級

05

031

- Instructions: Read the article below and summarize it in your own words as far as possible in English.
- Suggested length: 60-70 words
- Write your summary in the space provided on your answer sheet. <u>Any writing outside the space will not be graded.</u>

An AI chatbot is a service that uses AI machine learning to automatically present appropriate answers to chat questions. The introduction of AI chatbots in marketing has helped greatly improve campaign performances. This market is expected to grow from $2.6 billion in 2019 to $9.4 billion by 2024.

Chatbots are available 24/7 and can respond instantly to questions from customers. They can also communicate with website visitors and social media followers in real-time. Additionally, they can be used to ask questions about customer preferences and adjust the service to the customer's needs accordingly.

However, as a drawback, chatbots cannot grasp the user's emotions. In fact, they may not be possible to understand how the user they are chatting with is feeling. This can make the chatbot appear emotionally insensitive and damage the brand's reputation. In addition, it is difficult to respond to long questions that even humans find difficult to answer. When communication breaks down, it is necessary to devise ways for the customer to talk with human staff, such as connecting the customer to a call center.

解 答 欄

5

準
1
級

10

06

15

20

033

● Instructions: Read the article below and summarize it in your own words as far as possible in English.

● Suggested length: 60-70 words

● Write your summary in the space provided on your answer sheet. <u>Any writing outside the space will not be graded.</u>

A thrift shop is a form of retail store where used clothes, furniture, home appliances, etc, are collected through donations and resold, with the proceeds donated to charitable activities. There were about 30,000 thrift shops in the US in 2023. Generally, the shops are primarily run by charitable organizations and staffed by volunteers. Therefore, whether you donate, buy, or work in the shop, everyone involved contributes to charity.

Thrift shops are filled with a wide variety of clothing styles, furniture and homewares. You can save a large amount of money by shopping there because everything is reasonably priced. More importantly, the more you use thrift shops, the more you help save the environment.

Despite these advantages, there are some drawbacks. As is the case with secondhand stores in general, no warranty is provided for anything purchased at a thrift shop. For example, a thrift shop stereo could last a lifetime, or it could break in a day. The one-year warranty you usually get when you buy from a retail store is not included with items bought at a thrift shop.

解 答 欄

5

10

15

20

準1級

07

035

- Instructions: Read the article below and summarize it in your own words as far as possible in English.
- Suggested length: 60-70 words
- Write your summary in the space provided on your answer sheet. <u>Any writing outside the space will not be graded.</u>

Certain forms of recycling can be used on certain types of waste. These include material recycling, which reuses waste as raw materials for new products, and chemical recycling, which converts waste into other substances through chemical synthesis and uses those substances as raw materials to create new products. However, some materials cannot be recycled in these ways. Instead, these materials undergo thermal recycling, which is a method that recovers and utilizes the heat generated when burning waste. When these materials are burned, the energy created is called "thermal energy." According to the Ministry of Economy, Trade and Industry, 63% of the total waste plastic discarded in Japan in 2022 was processed by means of thermal recycling.

This is beneficial because when plastic breaks down, it generates methane gas, one of the greenhouse gases that promote global warming. Methane gas is said to have a greenhouse effect more than 20 times that of carbon dioxide. Thermal recycling can suppress the generation of methane gas that accompanies the deterioration of plastics.

Thermal recycling is not a perfect solution, however. When waste is burned at a waste incineration plant, exhaust gases containing dioxins and other toxic substances are emitted. While thermal recycling suppresses the emission of methane gas, it does emit carbon dioxide, which is also bad for the environment.

解 答 欄

準
1
級

08

5

10

15

20

037

- Instructions: Read the article below and summarize it in your own words as far as possible in English.
- Suggested length: 60-70 words
- Write your summary in the space provided on your answer sheet. Any writing outside the space will not be graded.

Rather than having a pet, some people like to go to animal cafes. In fact, the number of such cafes has been increasing in recent years because they allow people who cannot have pets for some reasons to have close contact with animals.

These dog and cat cafes are popular for good reason —— playing with animals has been proven to enhance the mental and emotional health of people. Another benefit of these cafes is that they facilitate pet adoptions. By visiting these cafes, people are more likely to bond with the animals, increasing the likelihood of finding a home for them.

On the downside, long contact with strangers in the closed space of a cafe can put stress on the animals, which makes them more susceptible to disease. Furthermore, there are some animal cafes that use rare animals, such as owls and hedgehogs, obtained by smuggling. In fact, for the benefit of the health of the animals, this type of exotic pet cafe is illegal in Europe, the U.S., and Taiwan.

解　答　欄

5

準
1
級

10

15

09

20

039

- **Instructions: Read the article below and summarize it in your own words as far as possible in English.**
- **Suggested length: 60-70 words**
- **Write your summary in the space provided on your answer sheet. Any writing outside the space will not be graded.**

Since 2019, New Zealand has been using a well-being indicator to measure its national development. The indicator, called the Living Standards Framework, measures not only economic factors but also social, environmental, and cultural aspects of well-being. However, some people think that the well-being indicator is too vague and subjective.

Supporters of the well-being indicator say that it reflects the true values and priorities of the people. They argue that the well-being indicator can help the government make better policies that improve the quality of life for everyone. For example, the well-being indicator can guide the government to invest more in health, education, and environmental protection.

Although the well-being indicator has some supporters, critics have pointed out problems with it. They say that the well-being indicator is not reliable or consistent, as it depends on people's subjective feelings and opinions. Additionally, they claim that the well-being indicator can distract the government from focusing on economic growth and stability, which are essential for the country's development. They suggest that the well-being indicator should be used as a supplement, not a substitute, for traditional economic indicators.

解 答 欄

5

10

15

20

- Instructions: Read the article below and summarize it in your own words as far as possible in English.
- Suggested length: 90-110 words
- Write your summary in the space provided on your answer sheet. <u>Any writing outside the space will not be graded.</u>

Sea reclamation projects in Bahrain, where the seabed is used to build new islands, have been carried out mainly along the coastline since the 1960s, expanding the country from 690 square km to over 780 square km by 2021— making Bahrain today slightly larger in area than Singapore. Neighboring Gulf states with even larger land areas have also been building large-scale artificial islands for decades. Some are especially striking, such as Palm Jumeirah in Dubai, which started being constructed in 1990. It is now a group of offshore islands that together resemble a palm tree and are home to luxury hotels.

Meanwhile, experts studying the history of artificial island construction are concerned about the impact of projects to reclaim the sea and build islands. This is because these artificial islands are often built on coral reefs that are home to hundreds of tropical species. These reefs act as natural filters for the water, but the construction of artificial islands has reduced the area of this natural filter and has worsened the quality of the water in the Persian Gulf.

In Bahrain, 182,000 square meters of coral reefs have been lost as a result of frequent dredging of the sands of the seabed near Muharraq Island. Furthermore, 95% of the mangroves in Tubli Bay, which is located in the northeastern area of Bahrain Island, were also found to have been lost due to dredging in land reclamation projects. If the construction of these artificial islands continues, within the next decade, all of the shallow coastal areas will become land, and the offshore areas will become shallower, changing the environment of the Persian Gulf. However, in 2019, an order to ban the extracting and dredging of sand, in a bid to allow the kingdom's seabed to recover from decades of damage, was announced by Bahraini Prime Minister Prince Khalifa bin Salman Al Khalifa.

解 答 欄

5

10

15

1
級

01

20

- Instructions: Read the article below and summarize it in your own words as far as possible in English.
- Suggested length: 90-110 words
- Write your summary in the space provided on your answer sheet. <u>Any writing outside the space will not be graded.</u>

Currently, about 70 million tons of palm oil are produced annually worldwide. Three countries, namely Indonesia, Malaysia, and Thailand, are responsible for about 90% of this production. Palm oil is the most widely used vegetable oil in the world. Although its use in food products, mainly in processed foods such as bread and potato chips, accounts for 80% of its total use, palm oil is also used in detergents and is the main ingredient in soap. Over the past 10 years, in Indonesia, palm oil production has doubled and continues to increase. In particular, production of palm oil is the highest in the world on Indonesia's Sumatra Island.

However, compared to 30 years ago, the island's forests have been reduced to less than half, and lowland forests are almost gone. They have been cleared on a large scale to cultivate oil palms and have been transformed into oil palm plantations. Their exponential expansion on Sumatra Island has led to widespread deforestation, or the destruction of rainforests, and the displacement of wildlife, particularly orangutans. The continued damage to where they live has unfavorable outcomes, as they not only lose their homes but also confront escalating risks of starvation and dangerous encounters with humans, who poach them for food or to sell as pets. At present, the Sumatran orangutan is considered critically endangered, with an estimated population of only 6,600 individuals.

In order to ensure deforestation-free production, further reforestation is necessary, especially considering the growing global population. While there are alternatives to using palm oil, its unparalleled yield —6 to 10 times more than other oils— makes it a challenging switch. To address environmental concerns, a certification system for sustainable palm oil now strictly regulates its production, distribution, and sales. Consumers can contribute to environmental sustainability by choosing certified sustainable products.

解 答 欄

5

10

15

1
級

20

02

045

- Instructions: Read the article below and summarize it in your own words as far as possible in English.
- Suggested length: 90-110 words
- Write your summary in the space provided on your answer sheet. Any writing outside the space will not be graded.

When the Industrial Revolution began in the 1800s, companies felt little reason to maintain even basic hygiene, safety, or environmental standards. In such circumstances, it was not uncommon for workers to be maimed or killed. Children were also found in these workplaces, particularly in clothing factories. The worst of these businesses were nicknamed "sweatshops." By the mid-20th century, these workplace practices had seemingly ended. However, sweatshops had by no means disappeared. In 2024, the total value of the sweatshop sector was estimated to be US$1.5 trillion greater than ever before.

The sweatshops of today resemble their historical counterparts, but with important differences. Those in economies with strong labor and environmental laws tend to be fairly clandestine. Sometimes they even operate in obscure, unmarked buildings. Moreover, they often rely on undocumented workers from underdeveloped countries. Such workers are often scared of the local government and so will not lodge complaints no matter how badly they are abused. In some cases, sweatshop owners have ties to criminal gangs or corrupt police, giving the owners another layer of protection. These businesses are not only active in manufacturing but also in online fraud, human trafficking, and black market operations. Worldwide, an estimated 168 million children work in sweatshops, often in virtual slavery.

There are numerous labor, UN, and human rights organizations cracking down on sweatshops. However, the term "sweatshop" itself is contested. Some economists argue that, as long as the workers are free adults, there is no need for the government to impose regulations. Particularly in regions plagued with extreme poverty, any factory—even one operating well below Western standards—can provide valuable sources of local income. Nevertheless, many activists, union leaders and politicians continue to demand that sweatshops either improve their operating conditions or close down.

解 答 欄

5

10

15

1 級

20

03

- **Instructions: Read the article below and summarize it in your own words as far as possible in English.**
- **Suggested length: 90-110 words**
- **Write your summary in the space provided on your answer sheet. <u>Any writing outside the space will not be graded.</u>**

Millions of children in West and Central Africa still lack access to education. Instead of studying, these children are typically engaged in various forms of labor. For instance, in Tanzania, 22.3% of children aged 5 to 14 are engaged in economic activities, from agriculture to mining. This is not always because parents prefer their children to work, but often because there is a dearth of options open to them.

These areas—often remote—lack both schools and teachers, and a UN assessment notes that even when teachers are available, they are often poorly trained or not trained at all. This leaves children with no choice but to become manual laborers early in life. This results in a net loss for national and regional development since an educated workforce is necessary for industrialization and modernization. In fact, even basic economic advancement requires a workforce with at least an elementary level of schooling.

In parts of Africa, material educational challenges are exacerbated by gender inequalities. As in much of the developing world, there is a strong preference for boys among many African families, and if they have resources to spend on education, boys will usually receive that education instead of girls: in Niger, 70% of poor girls receive no education at all, meaning that they can contribute almost nothing to the national economy. Mothers without formal education are also an issue. UNESCO's research indicates that the first 1,000 days of life are critical for a child's physical, mental, and educational growth, including early literacy, numeracy and social skills. However, poorly educated mothers are unable to provide these skills. This is therefore a crucial problem to be addressed, considering that providing women with educational opportunities brings great returns to the state, educated girls significantly increase the country's GDP and educated mothers are able to raise healthier children.

解 答 欄

5

10

15

20

1
級

04

- **Instructions: Read the article below and summarize it in your own words as far as possible in English.**
- **Suggested length: 90-110 words**
- **Write your summary in the space provided on your answer sheet. Any writing outside the space will not be graded.**

Venezuela was once known as one of the great resort areas of the Caribbean and had some of the largest oil reserves in the world. Also, it used to be a rich country that accepted refugees from many nations. However, the humanitarian crisis in Venezuela has escalated to become the second largest in the world, following the long-standing conflict in Syria, making it the largest refugee crisis in South America. Since 2014, more than 7.3 million Venezuelans have left the country, with 20 percent of the population having departed, due to poverty and worsening security situations. In fact, as of September 2023, there were 7.7 million refugees and migrants forced to flee their homes.

Years of economic mismanagement and corruption under former president, Hugo Chávez played a major role in the substantial reduction of oil production and profits. Furthermore, the drop in global oil prices in 2014 led to a rapid economic decline. Consequently, Venezuela has been suffering from hyperinflation since the end of 2017, when the inflation rate rose to a frightening 1.3 million percent per year. As a result, people in Venezuela could not survive, and many, including many in the indigenous population, were compelled to leave for other countries. The loss of social order has led to widespread violence and a declining economic state, resulting in shortages of food, clothing, medicine, and other necessities.

Latin American countries, such as Colombia, Peru, and Ecuador, are hosting many Venezuelan refugees. Colombia, in particular, has become home to the highest number of them, with a minimum of 2.9 million refugees. Despite the ongoing economic crisis, many of the Venezuelan refugees have expressed a desire to return home. Recently, an increasing number of people have decided to return to their homeland.

解答欄